UBLASAUN

First Light

In the Inupiaq language Ublasaun means first light
or when dawn is breaking.
-- Lawrence Kaplan, Alaska Native Language Center,
University of Alaska Fairbanks

~ Ublasaun is depicted on these two pages as interpreted by James Creech.

~ Cover image by James Kivetoruk Moses. Photo by Trevor Roehl, courtesy of Alaska State Museum (VA-122).

View from Devil Mountain, an ancient shield volcano in the Bering Land Bridge National Preserve.
~~ Photo by Vicky Goetchus and Mari Edwards.

Inupiaq Hunters and Herders in the Early Twentieth Century,

Northern Seward Peninsula, Alaska

UBLASAUN

First Light

Prepared by the Alaska System Support Office
U.S. Department of the Interior, National Park Service
Alaska Field Area
Shared Beringian Heritage Program

December 1996

Jeanne Schaaf, Content and Photo Editor
Thetus Smith, Copy and Layout Editor

Some of the photographic material used in this book is copyrighted
by the photographers or owners of the material.

ISBN 0-941555-02-X

CONTENTS

INTRODUCTION   1
~ Jeanne Schaaf

ACKNOWLEDGMENTS   5

THE BERING LAND BRIDGE - EARLY RESEARCH   18
~ David M. Hopkins

BEFORE OUR FATHERS' TIME - LATE PREHISTORIC INUPIAT
   of the NORTHERN SEWARD PENINSULA   42
~ Jeanne Schaaf

The HOPE and PROMISE of UBLASAUN   62
~ Susan W. Fair, James Creech, Gideon K. Barr Sr., and Edgar Ningeulook

HISTORICAL ARCHAEOLOGY and the EARLY TWENTIETH CENTURY
   REINDEER HERDING FRONTIER on the NORTHERN SEWARD PENINSULA   94
~ S. Craig Gerlach

TALES and PLACES, TOPONYMS, and HEROES   110
~ Susan W. Fair

ILAGANIQ, a FOLKTALE   126
~ Gideon K. Barr Sr.

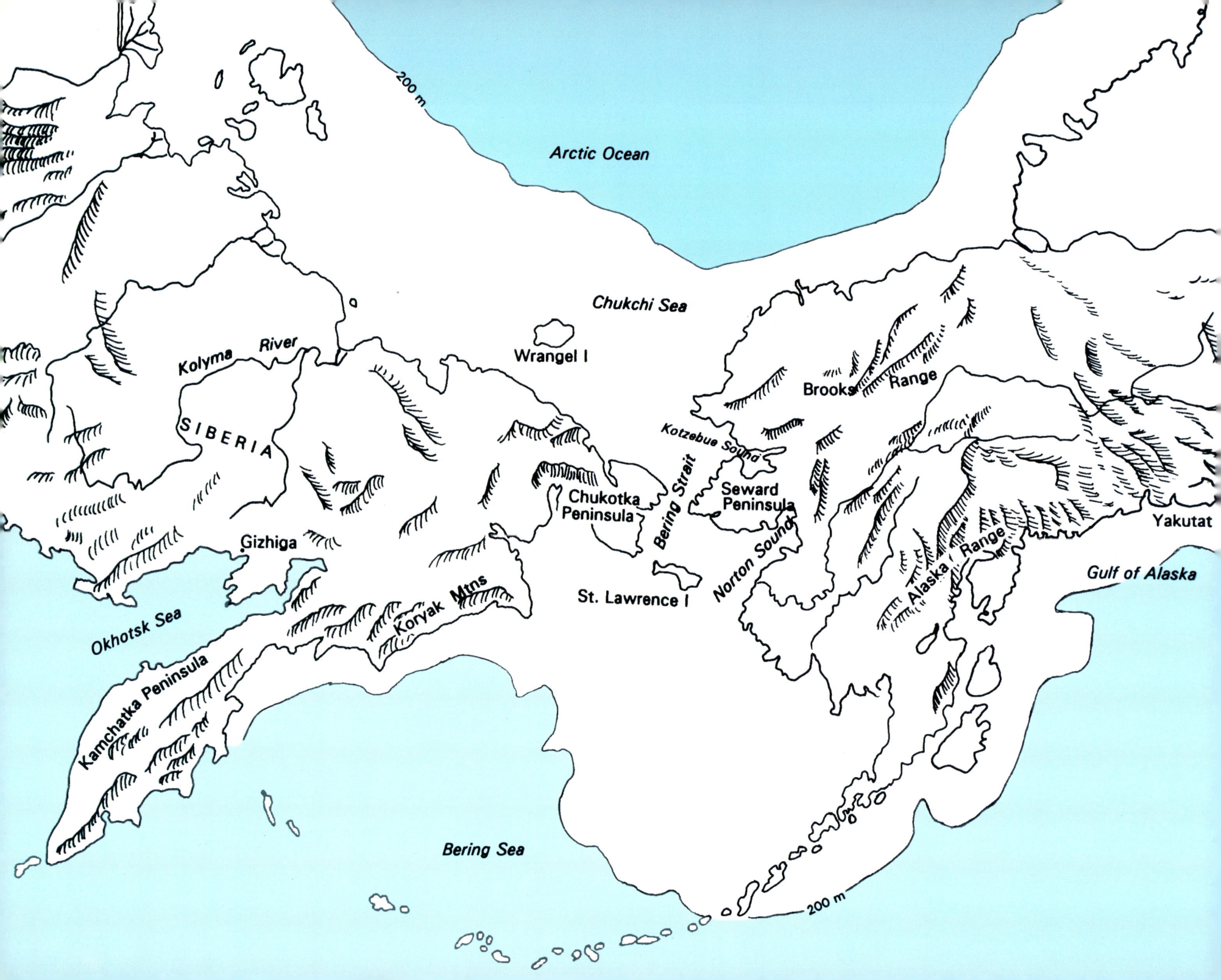

*You have to watch what grows...
They (the ancestors) watch the land.*

*They put away anything that is edible for the coming winter so they won't go hungry.
Just the same, sometimes they go hungry when the weather is bad...*

~ Gideon K. Barr Sr. 1993

(Map, opposite page)
The maximum extent of the Bering Land Bridge and several locations mentioned in the text.

INTRODUCTION

Near the center of what was once a vast ice-age "bridge" between the Old and New Worlds lies the Seward Peninsula of Alaska. During a series of ice ages beginning 2.3 million years ago, low sea levels exposed the shallow floors of the northern Bering Sea, Bering Strait, and Chukchi Sea, transforming the shores of the Seward Peninsula into high ground, several hundred kilometers inland from the ice-age coasts and rising above an expansive lowland plain dissected by now-submerged river systems. Conversely, melting of continental ice masses during warm climates brought higher sea levels, and during exceptionally warm periods they carved shorelines well inland from today's northern Seward Peninsula coast.

The story of the Bering Land Bridge and the complex history of human-landscape interaction played out on its stage are deciphered from fossils and artifacts preserved in ancient sediments and sites. Like the pages of a journal, this story is read from the layers of the earth comprising the modern landscape; the geomorphology, the remains of prehistoric cultures, the structure of modern biotic communities, and the memories and lives of the Inupiaq people. This unique record of landscape and biogeographic history provides unparalleled opportunities to investigate past and present climate change, as well as biotic and cultural exchanges and evolution. In recognition of the outstanding scientific value of the area, the northern one-third of the Seward Peninsula was set aside by presidential proclamation in 1980 as the Bering Land Bridge National Preserve.

I first visited the remote landscape of the former land bridge and became aware of its rich cultural, natural, and geological history more than a decade ago as a National Park Service archaeologist, employed with others to inventory cultural sites. The former land bridge has a subtle, powerful beauty that quietly draws you in. On the coast near Ikpik we witnessed the overnight transition in late June from a seemingly lifeless frozen ice-scape to one teeming with life-sustaining resources. The dense spring fog lifted one day to reveal shore-fast ice, cracked by leads and dotted with hundreds of seals. The air was filled with the calls of migrating birds where there had been silence the day before. We saw flock after flock of Sandhill cranes arrive from wintering grounds thousands of miles to the south and watched northbound whales spouting against the silhouetted Diomede Islands.

With the southward migrations at the end of our short field season in late August, the land seemed to fall silent again. While documenting the remains of abandoned camps, villages, monuments, and caches, and noting scatters of bones from a great variety of sea and terrestrial animals, we were constantly reminded of the Inupiaq ancestors' strength and ingenuity and the absolute necessity of putting away stores of food from late spring through freeze-up, to ensure winter survival.

Through Dave Hopkins, Professor Emeritus of Quaternary Studies at the University of Alaska Fairbanks and pioneer of Bering Land Bridge research, I met Gideon Kahlook Kunautaq Barr Sr. Mr. Barr is an Inupiaq elder and historian originally from Cape Espenberg and who later resided in Shishmaref. He helped interpret the results of our survey by identifying historic sites, sharing details such as names, dates, activities, and folktales associated with sites that we had recorded. He painted the landscape with a rich and colorful layer of place names and stories about past events, revealing places on the landscape holding deep cultural significance - places often not visible in the archaeological record.

Mr. Barr's keen interest in Inupiaq history and his life-long dedication to the preservation of traditional knowledge were catalysts in launching a five-year study called the One Man's Heritage Project -- the subject of this book.

Ublasaun, meaning first light or when dawn is breaking, is a place on the northern Seward Peninsula coast, between Shishmaref and Cape Espenberg. Now an archaeological site "discovered" by our inventory, Ublasaun was once Gideon Barr's boyhood home - the winter village of reindeer herders in the early twentieth century. Long before memory it was also home to prehistoric seal hunters. Ublasaun was the focal point of the One Man's Heritage Project, a long-term, integrated study of the human ecology, ethnohistory, ethnoarchaeology, and historic architecture of early twentieth century Inupiaq reindeer herders. The content of that multidisciplinary study is represented in part by the essays and photographs in this book. The One Man's Heritage Project has resulted in many publications and manuscripts, as well as the release of a companion videotape entitled *Siulipta Paitaat: Our Ancestors' Heritage*, narrated primarily by Gideon Barr, his sister Bessie Barr Cross, and Dave Hopkins.

Dave Hopkins' essay describing early research on the Bering Land Bridge provides an introduction to the land and the process of scientific discovery of its forgotten past. His essay also touches upon other landscape history studies funded by the National Park Service under the auspices of the Shared Beringian Heritage Program, described below.

"Before our fathers' time," as Gideon refers to the realm of prehistory, is a discussion of archaeological investigations at late prehistoric sites dating from AD 1500 to 1800. During that time, an interesting picture emerges on the northern Seward Peninsula. By the 1700s we see people on the move, changes in settlement patterns, and construction of

(Opposite page)
Late-prehistoric house depressions on ancient beach ridges at the tip of Cape Espenberg. The white mark at the left is Ilaganiq's whale bone cairn. ~ Photo by James Magdanz.

> *Where people have been living in early days, like this camp that I'm talking about at Espenberg, Ilaganiq's camp. That old site is real valuable to me, to what I think. I'm concerned about his whaling equipment, what he used to kill his whale, harpoon tips, whatever. What he used to kill that big of a whale just by using his own handmade hunting equipment. Something got to be sharp and good in order to kill that big of a whale according to the size of the head that is displayed on the top of the earth right alongside the old, old houses there. That's why I value those old houses... Those old sites are so valuable to my understanding, 'cause there's some thing that the ancestors made which we don't even see and use ourselves anymore.*
>
> *That's a valuable part of it right there. How they have survived with their handmade tools, hunting equipment like that in order to survive, before white people bring their guns in and their iron and stuff like that.*
>
> ~ Gideon K. Barr Sr. 1987

monumental architecture, possibly reflecting territorial defense and conflict in resource-rich boundary zones during a time of accelerated trade and climatic deterioration. The turn of the nineteenth century is also significant because it represents the time immediately before commercial whaling in the Bering Strait and the subsequent decline of key marine resources, before the population decline and collapse of traditional Inupiaq societies, before the disappearance of caribou from the Seward Peninsula, and before the widespread availability of European manufactured goods. These are the last Inupiat living in "bow and arrow" time as Gideon Barr would say, engaged in Siberian trade and perched on the cusp of tremendous culture change.

The essay about Ublasaun takes a look at early twentieth century life at the community built by Gideon's father Makaiqtaq Barr, his family and kinsmen as they merged traditional subsistence practices with newly introduced reindeer herding. Mr. Barr's detailed knowledge of house construction techniques, village layout, the occupants and their relationships to one another, and site activities, coupled with on-site investigations by architects and archaeologists, enabled National Park Service historic architects Steve Peterson and James Creech to produce the first architectural renderings of historic Native structures in Alaska.

"Historical Archaeology and the Early Twentieth Century Reindeer Herding Frontier on the Northern Seward Peninsula, Alaska" by S. Craig Gerlach is taken from a manuscript in progress with the same working title. It summarizes ethnohistorical and historic archaeological investigations at Ublasaun and other historic sites utilized by the Barr family in the early part of this century. This study examines the question of how the reindeer herding economy was integrated with the subsistence economy of the early 1900s at the local family level. Although many Inupiat in Northwest Alaska participated in reindeer herding, they did not abandon their traditional hunter-gatherer lifestyle to become pastoralists, as intended by the government agents administering the program.

Susan W. Fair's essay, "Tales and Places, Toponyms, and Heroes" introduces a folktale narrated by Gideon Barr about strongman and hero, Ilaganiq, considered by Barr to be a direct ancestor. Her essay, as well as many of the photographs that appear in this book, draw from her research and manuscript entitled *Qamani: Up the Coast in My Mind, in My Heart: Inupiaq History and Heritage in Bering Land Bridge National Preserve*, co-authored with Edgar Ningeulook of Shishmaref. *Qamani* is a comprehensive work intended to introduce readers to the One Man's Heritage Project research and to Inupiaq life and history in the northern Seward Peninsula region. The Ilaganiq folktale represents a piece of the rich oral history remembered for future generations by Gideon Barr, a history that recalls what the ancestors accomplished and which serves to bolster spirit and pride, linking the Inupiat then and now.

~ Jeanne Schaaf

Gideon Barr explains his father's reindeer diary to pilot M.O. Olson, July 1991.
~ Photo by Jeanne Schaaf.

REFERENCES

Schaaf, J. M.
1992   The Shared Beringian Heritage Program. *Federal Archeology Report* 5(2):1-3.

1995   Understanding northern environments and human populations through cooperative research: a case study in Beringia. In *Human Ecology and Climate Change: People and Resources in the Far North*. D. L. Peterson and D. R. Johnson (eds.) Taylor and Francis, Washington, D.C.

ACKNOWLEDGMENTS

The One Man's Heritage Project is just one part of a larger National Park Service research program called the Shared Beringian Heritage Program spearheaded by NPS Acting Deputy Director Denis P. Galvin. This program was initiated in 1991 by Paul Haertel and Terje (Ted) Birkedal at the National Park Service Alaska Regional Office (now the Alaska System Support Office) to illustrate and promote the kind of scientific exchanges and partnerships that would be nurtured by a joint Russian-American Beringian Heritage International Park (Schaaf 1992, 1995). This ongoing program unites Russian and American scientists, land managers, and Native people in a long-term, multidisciplinary research effort focused on the study of traditional lifeways, biogeography, paleoenvironment, and landscape history in Northwest Alaska and Northeastern Siberia.

Many people on staff at the University of Alaska Fairbanks and at the National Park Service in Anchorage and Nome, as well as the people of Shishmaref contributed to the One Man's Heritage Project in countless ways, too numerous to name here. Dale Taylor deserves special mention for his unflagging support of diverse and integrated research. A work in progress entitled *From Hunters to Herders: The Transformation of Earth, Society, and Heaven Among the Inupiat of Beringia* by Linda J. Ellanna and George Sherrod, is a central piece of the One Man's Heritage Project and was drawn upon by the other ethnohistoric studies. Segments of interviews with Dave Hopkins and Gideon Barr conducted and videotaped by Francine Taylor are reproduced here.

James Magdanz took several of the photographs used here for the One Man's Heritage Project. Chris Arend photographed collections at the Anchorage Museum of History and Art, as did Trevor Roehl at F-Stop Photo in Juneau through the Alaska State Museum, courtesy respectively of curators Walter Van Horn and Steve Henrickson.

Richard Keithahn of Lopez Island, Washington allowed the NPS to duplicate photographs taken by his father Edward Keithahn in the early 1920s when his father and mother Toni were teachers in Shishmaref. As a result of Richard Keithahn's generosity and interest, the National Park Service gave an album of more than 200 historic photographs from this collection to Shishmaref, where people can view and duplicate them. Several photographs were loaned from the private collections of Charles Lucier and David Hopkins and from the records of the researchers participating in the One Man's Heritage Project.

***

S. Craig Gerlach records the eroding remains of camps occupied in prehistoric times at Ublasaun, July 1991.

~ Photo by Jeanne Schaaf.

I've always seen Gideon as a Native scholar. I feel there's a considerable similarity between me and Gideon. We certainly come from different backgrounds, but I can imagine if I were born in Shishmaref, I'd be a person much like Gideon ... driven by a compelling necessity to preserve knowledge.

~ David M. Hopkins

Gideon Kahlook Barr Sr. revisited his boyhood home at Ublasaun with National Park Service archaeologists, September 1990.
~ Photo by Jeanne Schaaf.

David M. Hopkins conducts thaw lake research near the Kitluk River, Bering Land Bridge National Preserve, August 1995.
~ Photo by Jeanne Schaaf.

Gideon Barr leans against parts of a shipwreck incorporated into the entryway of a sod house used around 1918 at Qivilauq (Kividlo) as he assists NPS archaeologist Jeanne Schaaf taking measurements of the amount of land lost to erosion, September 1990. ~ Photo by Terje Birkedal.

In prehistoric times musk oxen roamed the land bridge, a landscape that may have looked much like the present day Bering Land Bridge National Preserve. ~~ Photo by Jeanne Schaaf.

Gideon Barr and Bessie Barr Cross returned to their childhood home at Espenberg in August 1993. They are sitting outside the sod house that he built for their mother in the 1940s.
~~ Photo by Edgar Ningeulook.

**Bessie (Elizabeth) Barr Cross
remembers her childhood on the beach at Ublasaun,
August 1993.**
~ Photo by Jeanne Schaaf.

Gideon Barr (right) explains to NPS historic architect Jim Creech that support beams, floor planks, and other horizontal members were leveled using the expansive horizon of the sea as a reference, July 1991.
~ Photo by Jennifer Kramer.

Gideon Barr (center) describes aspects of the construction of his boyhood home, now in ruins, at Ublasaun to NPS historic architect Jim Creech (left) and anthropologist Igor Krupnik (right), July 1991.
~ Photo by Jennifer Kramer.

Herbert O. Anungazuk, pictured here, assisted Peter Richter in mapping Ublasaun, July 1991.
~~ Photo by Peter Richter.

Susan W. Fair and Edgar Ningeulook (second from left) interview Gideon and Fannie Barr in their Shishmaref home, August 1993.
~ Photo by James Magdanz.

Fannie Kigrook Barr, wife of Gideon Barr, is an accomplished skinsewer who had many mentors -- among them her mother, Annie Tocktoo, and Gideon's mother, Emily Barr. Here she discusses a fancy parka Gideon commissioned for her from Ethel Washington, a renowned seamstress from Kotzebue. Barr trapped the squirrels for the parka himself; and his mother, Emily Barr, pieced the calfskin border. The parka thus combines the talents of several households and generations. -- Photo by James Magdanz, August 1993.

Shishmaref elders Davey and Frieda Ningeulook examine an album of Edward Keithahn's photographs, which was reprinted from the Keithahn negatives for Shishmaref by the National Park Service, courtesy of Keithahn's son Richard. Many elders assisted in identification of the photographs, which brought back memories of their first days in school, of long-deceased friends and relatives, and of the teacher they called "Qatuk."
~ Photo by James Magdanz, August 1993.

(Above left) Teacher Edward Keithahn circa 1923, whose photo collection forms the most extensive survey available on Shishmaref area life during the first half of this century. (Above right) Al Allockeok, Elsie Allockeok (Weyiouanna), Kara Allockeok (Ahgupuk), and teacher Toni Keithahn pose with captured swans. ~~ Photos courtesy of Richard Keithahn and National Park Service (neg. 135 and neg. 077).

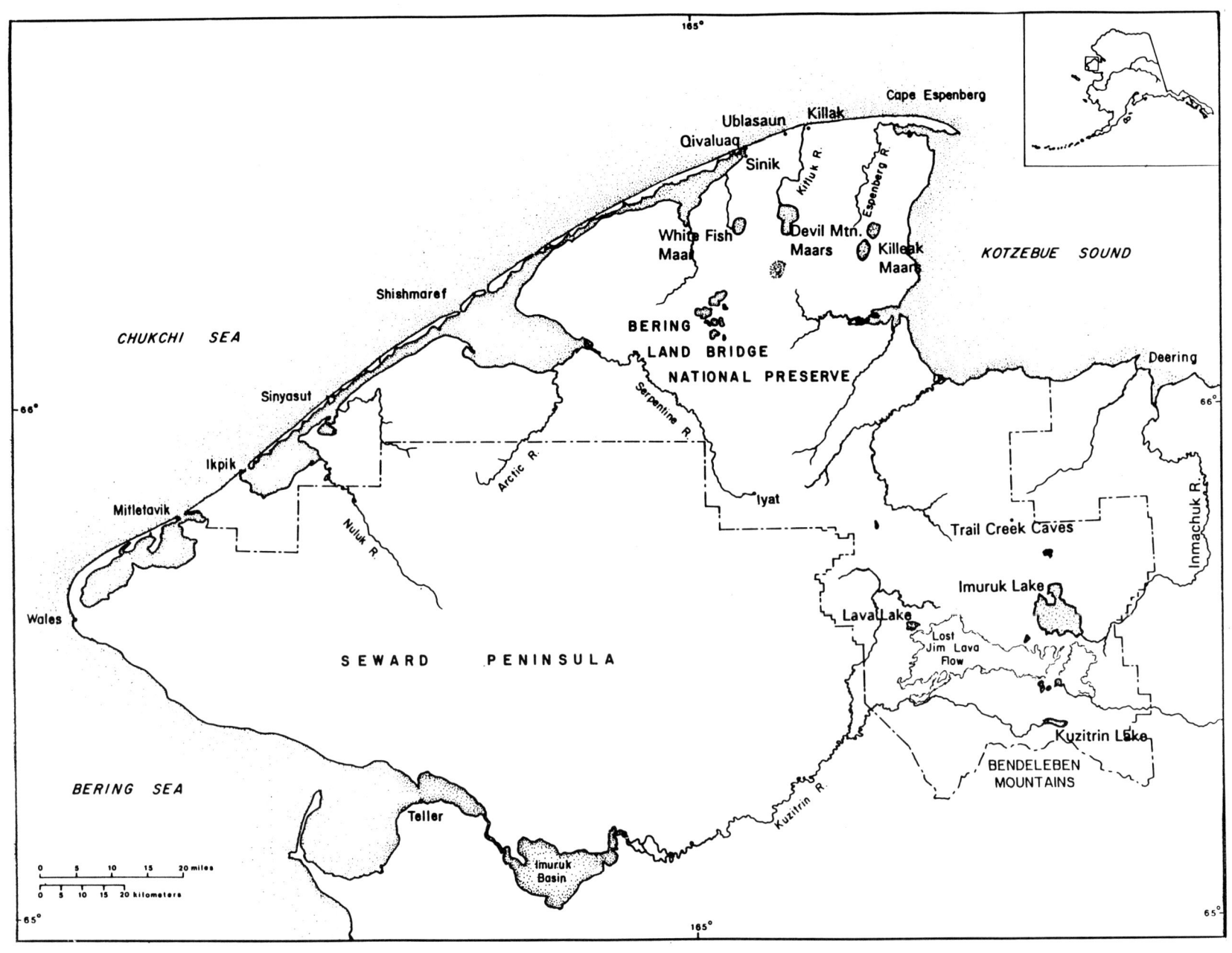

Map of Bering Land Bridge National Preserve showing locations of places mentioned in the following texts.

The Bering Land Bridge

Early Research

North America and Asia come close to meeting on the Arctic Circle -- so close, in fact, that Cape Dezhnev, the easternmost mountain in Asia, can easily be seen from the top of Cape Mountain, the westernmost mountain of mainland North America. Alaska and Siberia are separated, nowadays, by cold, turbulent, and often icy seas; but the Bering Strait forms a bottleneck so narrow that it once seemed the logical site for a telegraph line from New York to Moscow. Efforts to build the Russian-American Telegraph line were abandoned only after the first intercontinental cable was successfully laid beneath the Atlantic Ocean.

So close are the two continents at the Bering Strait, that tens of thousands of North American waterfowl cross annually to fatten up on the verdant summer tundra of Chukotka (northeasternmost Siberia), while a variety of songbirds migrate in the opposite direction, coming from India and Southeast Asia to nest and raise their young while exploiting the summer resources of the tundra of northern Alaska. How did these intercontinental migration patterns come about? Do bird genes retain a memory of a landscape in which Chukotka and Alaska were joined? Paradoxically, Bering Strait also provides an avenue for seasonal north-south migrations, most notably by walrus and bowhead, gray, and beluga whales that follow the retreating sea ice to take advantage of a summer flush of productivity in the shallow waters of the Chukchi and Beaufort Seas.

The Chukchi Sea and the northeastern half of the Bering Sea -- seas that separate Alaska from northeastern Siberia -- are both quite shallow, for they are simply sunken parts of continents. They are parts of a former land bridge that began to subside several million years ago during the Pliocene epoch. The outermost edges of this former land bridge now lie as much as 200 meters (about 650 feet) below today's sea level. The land bridge was a barrier to marine migrations between the Pacific and the Arctic Oceans, and the first indications that the land bridge had submerged and that Bering Strait had come into existence are provided by ancient fossil clams of Pacific ancestry found in distant places, such as Meighan Island on the Canadian shores of the Arctic Ocean and the Tjornes Peninsula of Iceland in the North Atlantic. Equally ancient fossil clam shells and seal bones of Atlantic ancestry are found near Yakutat on the coast of Southeast Alaska and on Karagin Island, off the coast of the Kamchatka Peninsula; they indicate that the Bering Land Bridge first became submerged more than 3 million years ago.

Slow submergence had caused the outlines of the Alaska and Siberia coasts to take nearly their present shape when the ice ages began, some 2.3 million years ago. Most of the Seward Peninsula remained emergent, for example, although its north shore lay at the inner edge of the broad coastal plain now

One of the things I enjoyed about working not only with Gideon, but also with other Inupiaq people, is finding out a lot about the landscape that I didn't know to begin with... of learning nuances that I didn't see.

~ David M. Hopkins
University of Alaska Fairbanks - Emeritus

occupied by the northern part of the Bering Land Bridge National Preserve. Today the sites of Cape Espenberg, the village of Shishmaref, and Ublasaun, where a youthful Gideon Barr watched over his reindeer, actually lay several tens of kilometers offshore.

Global climates were steadily cooling during the Pliocene epoch, and consequently, tundra -- the treeless vegetation of the north -- was just beginning to appear on the most northern islands of Canada. A striking picture of Bering Land Bridge vegetation could be seen a few years ago in the Lava Camp gold mine in the Inmachuk River valley near Deering, Alaska. Here, in a small tunnel excavated beneath a 5-million-year-old basaltic lava flow, one could see the roots and stumps of a flood-plain forest that had been buried and partly burned beneath the encroaching lava. When this Pliocene basalt invaded the Inmachuk River valley, the Seward Peninsula and the nearby land bridge were clothed in a rich and diverse coniferous forest of spruce, larch, hemlock, and pine interspersed with birch and poplar trees and alder and willow shrubs. In those days, animals of the northern forest could move back and forth across the land bridge between Old World Asia and New World North America; circumpolar boreal faunas must have been as uniform as circumpolar arctic faunas are today.

With the beginning of the ice ages, roughly 2.3 million years ago, the history of the Bering Land Bridge began to be complicated by sea-level fluctuations that resulted from the repeated growth and shrinkage of continental glaciers. Glaciers and ice caps represent substantial amounts of water stored on land. During cold periods, snow falling on mountains and plateaus fails to run back into the sea; glaciers grow into ice caps, and sea level falls. When the ice caps melt, water is returned to the sea, and sea level rises once again. At times when large continental ice caps expanded to cover much of North America, northern Europe, and northwestern Siberia, sea level fell 100 to 150 meters (330 to 500 feet), enough to bring a broad Bering Land Bridge back into existence -- a land bridge that stretched, at times, from St. Matthew Island in the Bering Sea to Wrangel Island in the Chukchi Sea. This happened at least 10 times during the past 800,000 years and perhaps many times more during the interval between 0.8 and 2.3 million years ago.

In a warm period on the other hand, if the entire Greenland ice cap were to melt, sea level would rise about 7 meters (about 25 feet); this actually happened about 125,000 years ago. If the Antarctic ice cap were also to melt, then sea level would rise more than 30 meters (100 feet); this also actually happened during an exceptionally warm period about 400,000 years ago. Old shorelines marking these and other periods of past high sea level can be seen in many coastal areas of Alaska and Chukotka, including parts of the Bering Land Bridge National Preserve.

Because the Pleistocene ice sheets were inherently unstable and constantly changing in size and volume, sea level was equally unstable, and the shores of the Bering Land Bridge were constantly changing. After reaching a temporary maximum width and area 18,000 years ago, the Bering Land Bridge rapidly narrowed as ice caps shrank and sea level rose. By 10,000 years ago, the Alaska-Siberia land connection had been reduced to a narrow isthmus only a few kilometers wide, extending from the western tip of St. Lawrence Island to the southeastern corner of the Chukchi Peninsula. By 9,500 years ago, this last land connection was severed by the continuing post-glacial rise in sea level.

The land bridge was probably never forested again after the first, prolonged episode of submergence that ended 2.3 million years ago. Instead, a wide belt of tundra or a drier treeless vegetation termed "tundra-steppe" separated Asian and North American forests on the many occasions that land connections were renewed during the past 2.3 million years. This limited the ability of forest-loving animals to disperse from one continent to the other; instead, a series of open-country animals, often grazers like antelope and elk, increasingly dominated the exchange.

During the latter part of the ice ages, animal dispersals across the Bering Land Bridge left a clear record in the form of fossil bones of mammoth, bison, elk, saiga (a small antelope that survives today in Kazakhstan and the Ukraine), and even lions, cheetahs, and saber-tooth cats. These bones are constantly washing out from Pleistocene (ice age) deposits exposed in the riverbanks and shoreline bluffs of the Bering Land Bridge National Preserve and other parts of the Seward Peninsula. The peculiar trans-Beringian migration paths of many of today's populations of cranes, ducks, geese, and songbirds must also have been established in land-bridge times.

Among the relatively late migrants across the Bering Strait were humans. Judging from evidence elsewhere in Alaska, the earliest people were hunter-gatherers who seem to have appeared in Chukotka no earlier than 13,000 years ago and then spread onto the narrowing land bridge and into Alaska. From there, these hunters rapidly colonized the rest of the Americas, becoming the ancestors of most American Indians. Another wave of migration about 10,000 years ago (shortly before the land bridge submerged) brought the ancestors of some and perhaps all of the Native peoples of northwestern North America. These wanderers left a record of their presence at Trail Creek Caves, an important archaeological site on the Bering Land Bridge Preserve. Many archaeologists and physical anthropologists believe that this early migration involved the ancestors of Dene speakers -- the Athabascans, the Navajos, and related groups who live mostly in Alaska and northwestern Canada -- and that the Eskimo ancestors of Gideon Barr, as well as the Aleuts, are descended from a third and much later wave of migrants that brought still another Asian population to the coastal fringe of Alaska about 4,000 years ago. Recent DNA studies, however, seem to indicate that Dene speakers and Eska-Aleuts are very closely related and are both descendants of the last group to migrate over the land bridge about 10,000 years ago. In any case, archaeological sites recording the past 4,000 years of Eskimo prehistory abound throughout the area of the Bering Land Bridge Preserve.

Although speculations about the possible former existence of a Bering Land Bridge date back to the late eighteenth century, serious research began only a few decades ago. My own interest was awakened when I was assigned, as a young U. S. Geological Survey geologist, to study the volcanic basalt plateau that covers a large area around Imuruk Lake. I was joined by Robert Sigafoos, an ecological botanist, who described the flora and the vegetation; together, we described the interaction of vegetation with frost-action and permafrost. Building on our studies, P.A. Colinvaux came to Imuruk Lake in 1957 to recover a core of the lake sediments. It proved impossible to core the stiff sediments on the floor of this large lake in the summer from a wind-tossed raft, so Colinvaux returned the following winter and bravely undertook Alaska's and possibly the world's first winter lake-coring operation. This effort produced Beringia's most remarkable pollen record, a pollen core that makes it possible to reconstruct vegetation changes at the eastern entrance to the Bering Land Bridge throughout the past 150,000 years.

The uplands of the Seward Peninsula are very beautiful; and they are exciting to a geologist because trees are lacking, tall shrubs are scarce, and the structure of the magnificent landscape can be clearly seen, partly cloaked in green but partly appearing from a distance to be exposed bare rock. One day in 1947, a bush pilot named John Cross emerged from a SeaBee amphibious plane that he landed in front of our camp on Imuruk Lake and invited himself into our cook tent for coffee and a chat. John was interested in every aspect of the beautiful Seward Peninsula landscape and in the people that lived in it, and he began to relay to us knowledge about the country that he had picked up from Bessie Barr, his fiancee, later to be his wife, and from her brother, Gideon Barr. The Barr family was an Inupiaq (northern Eskimo) family who maintained a large reindeer herd at the mouth of the Espenberg River. Thus began a long and enjoyable acquaintance with John Cross, with Bessie Barr Cross, and later, with Gideon Barr.

One of the things that John told us during that first visit concerned some limestone caves in which Native hunters taking shelter from a storm had found bone and stone artifacts. Later that summer, John flew us over the caves. During the following summer, my young colleagues and I took a long backpacking trip, found the caves, and conducted the first test excavation at Trail Creek Caves. In 1949 and 1950 the Danish archaeologist, Helge Larsen, conducted ambitious excavations in the caves and found a variety of stone and well-preserved bone artifacts extending back nearly 10,000 years.

My interest in the Imuruk Lake area continued, and I revisited it several times during the decades since 1947. Meanwhile, in 1949 and 1950, a Navy air photo squadron flew the Seward Peninsula, in support of preparation of mile-to-the-inch maps to be published by the U.S. Geological Survey; thus, air photos covering the entire peninsula soon became available to me. On these photos, I noticed five large, oval lakes that looked very much like meteor craters scattered over the tundra southwest of Cape Espenberg. When an opportunity finally came to visit

... when I began to know Gideon, the culture was changing. The technology was changing. Dog teams disappeared. Gideon kept a dog team in order to both preserve the dogs and the knowledge of harnessing and sled-making and hunting and traveling with dogs. Gideon told me that some day they're going to run out of gasoline and they're going to need those dogs again. And summarily he told me that he continued to hunt seals with seal nets, which is a very complex operation involved in getting the net through one hole in the ice and threading it through another. One of the holes has to be a seal breathing hole. So not too surprisingly, few know how to set a seal net anymore. But Gideon does, and he continued to do it to preserve the technique, the technology.

~~ David Hopkins

these lakes on the ground in 1966, I discovered that they were maars (volcanic explosion craters), not meteor craters, as I had originally thought.

That same summer John Cross flew me in to the reindeer camp of the Barr family on the Espenberg River, and there for the first time I met with Gideon Barr. A quick, small-boat reconnaissance of the Espenberg River and a traverse of the coast near the mouth of the Kitluk River, followed by a 12-hour open boat trip from Espenberg to Deering with Fred Goodhope and Fannie Barr Goodhope convinced me that the frozen silts and sands exposed in freshly eroded riverbanks and shoreline bluffs of the Espenberg region contained a remarkable paleo-environmental record that should be studied as soon as possible.

In 1970, with Robert Rowland and my daughter, Chindi, I returned to spend several weeks exploring the coast and the small rivers in the area between Goodhope Bay and Shishmaref Lagoon. We studied the sediments in detail and sieved them for seeds, beetle parts, and other abundant small fossils. In the course of these weeks, we discovered that when each of the maars had erupted, the tundra had been blanketed by layers of tephra (volcanic ash): the result was that fragments of the vegetated landscape of the Bering Land Bridge lay frozen and preserved intact beneath the tephra from each explosion. Now, we have found areas of buried tundra that are 17,000, about 36,000, and more than 42,000 years old.

My studies and those of Larsen, Colinvaux, and Sigafoos led to the recognition that the Seward Peninsula preserves an exceptional record of the past landscapes and biotas at the eastern end of the former Bering Land Bridge. As a result, the Bering Land Bridge National Preserve was established in 1980 to encompass an area with invaluable paleo-environmental and archaeological resources. An archaeological survey of parts of the Bering Land Bridge Preserve was conducted by a party led by Roger Powers in 1974 and 1975 (Powers, Ketz, and Scott 1975), and in 1985 and 1986, Jeanne Schaaf initiated a more ambitious survey of most of the area of the preserve (Schaaf 1988).

Schaaf's survey led to a series of geomorphic and paleo-environmental studies in the region by faculty and students of the University of Alaska Fairbanks (Hopkins 1988; Hopkins and Kidd 1988; Jordan 1988; Mason 1988; Vinson 1988). The younger archaeological sites proved to be concentrated along the coast, and many of them were, and are, threatened by very vigorous coastal erosion. In response the National Park Service began a three-year archaeological testing program, directed by Roger Harritt, to recover information from eroding sites at Ikpik and Cape Espenberg (Harritt 1994). During the late 1980s and early 1990s, James Jordan used old and recent maps and air photos to measure rates of coastal erosion and studied the dynamics of the beaches and coastal barrier islands of the Bering Land Bridge National Preserve (Jordan 1988, 1990).

At Cape Espenberg, the coast has been prograding rather than eroding during the last 3,500 years, and a remarkable series of proto-Eskimo settlements are preserved on the older beach ridges. Owen Mason has worked out a history of periods of erosion and dune-building that have alternated with periods of rapid progradation due to the building of low beach ridges. He has shown that this record reflects small-scale climatic events that are otherwise difficult to perceive in the geological record of the Seward Peninsula (Mason 1991, 1993). Now, it is becoming evident from the work of Mason and Jordan that the beach ridges and barrier islands of the Bering Land Bridge Preserve also preserve a 4,000-year record of small oscillations in sea level (Mason and Jordan 1991, 1993). In 1987, Janet Kidd studied geomorphic and limnological processes that shape the sediments deposited in the thaw lakes (lakes formed by local thawing of permafrost) that cover much of the landscape in the Cape Espenberg region (Hopkins and Kidd 1988).

A second series of long-term archaeological, geomorphic, and paleoenvironmental studies was initiated in 1991 under the Shared Beringian Heritage Program of the Beringian Heritage International Park Initiative.

Steve Charron of the University of Massachusetts is preparing a surficial geologic map of the area between Goodhope Bay and Shishmaref Lagoon. In April 1993 he successfully collected a series of sediment cores from the North Killeak Lake maar (Charron 1993, 1994; Charron and Hopkins 1993). Patricia Heiser has undertaken the completion of the surficial map for the remainder of the area included within the Bering Land Bridge National Preserve. James Beget has initiated a sophisticated volcanological study of the Espenberg maars (Beget and Charron 1993; Beget, Hopkins, and Charron 1996; Beget and Mann 1992). His student, Kurt Yuengling, has just begun studies of the granite tor formations at Serpentine Hot Springs. Dan Mann and Mari Edwards are extending the loess (wind-blown silt) and thaw-lake sediment studies that I began in 1970 (Goetcheus et al. 1994); and Vicky Goetcheus and Claudi Hoefle have launched a detailed study of the soils and vegetation buried under tephra falls (Hoefle, Edwards, et al. 1994; Hoefle, Ping, et al. 1994). The beach ridge plain is underlain by permafrost, which has permitted the development of a unique wetland under study by Lawrence Plug (1993; Hopkins and Plug 1994).

Meanwhile, Craig Gerlach, James Simon, Mary Ann Sweeney, and Catherine Williams have been conducting a historical archaeological excavation of Ublasaun (Simon and Gerlach 1992), and other historic sites with the active and extensive consultation of Gideon himself.

Gideon Barr and his sister Bessie have been threads of continuity through all of my studies in the Kotzebue Sound area. Bessie's role, with her death in 1994, has now come to a close, but her contributions will live on in this book and in many other ways. Over the years, I had come to know her well and also slowly became acquainted with Gideon as we met, repeatedly, at the Goodhope reindeer camp, at John and Bessie Cross' home in Kotzebue, and once or twice at Gideon's home in Shishmaref. I value Gideon as a true scholar devoted to the preservation and transmission of oral traditions that he first learned during his childhood; devoted to conserving -- by doing -- skills such as seal-netting under the winter ice; and devoted, finally, to the lovely landscape in which he has always lived.

~~ David Hopkins

SOURCES

Beget, J. and S. Charron
1993   Morphology and bathymetry of Arctic maars, northern Seward Peninsula. *Alaska Volcano Observatory Newsletter* 2:16-17.

Beget, J., D. M. Hopkins, S. Charron
1996   The Largest Known Maars on Earth, Seward Peninsula, Northwest Alaska. *Arctic* 49:1:62-69.

Beget, J. and D. Mann
1992   Caldera formation by unusually large phreatomagmatic eruptions through permafrost in Arctic Alaska. *Eos* 73:6361.

Charron, S.D.
1993   Shared Beringian Heritage Project: Surficial Mapping and Lake Coring within the Cape Espenberg-Devil Mountain Region (BELA): Report on 1993 Lake Coring of North Killeak Lake. Report on file at National Park Service, Anchorage, Alaska, 10 pp.

1993a Bathymetry Maps for North Devil Mountain Lake, South Devil Mountain Lake, North Killeak Lake, and South Killeak Lake (Bering Land Bridge National Preserve). On file at National Park Service, Anchorage, March 1993.

1994   A 20,000 year magnetic susceptibility record from North Killeak Lake, Bering Land Bridge National Preserve, Western Alaska. *Current Research in the Pleistocene* 11:126-127.

Charron, S. D. and J. Brigham-Grette
1994   A New Glacial to Holocene Record from North Killeak Lake, Bering Land Bridge National Preserve, Alaska, *PALEO Times* 2:9.

Charron, S. D. and D. M. Hopkins
1993   Examination of a Recently Drained Thermokarst Lake, Bering Bridge National Preserve (BELA), Western Alaska: Implications for Thaw Lake Processes and Regional Quaternary Stratigraphy. Geological Society of America, Abstracts with Programs, 93:392.

Colinvaux, P. A.
1964   The Environment of the Bering Land Bridge. *Ecological Monograms*, 34:297-329.

1967   Quaternary Vegetational History of Arctic Alaska. In *The Bering Land Bridge*, D. M. Hopkins (ed.), pp. 47-90, Stanford University Press, California.

Goetcheus, V.G., D. M. Hopkins, M. E. Edwards, and D. H. Mann
1994 Window on the Bering Land Bridge: A 17,000 yr B.P. Paleosurface on the Seward Peninsula. *Current Research in the Pleistocene* 11:131-132.

Harritt, R.
1994 *Eskimo Prehistory on the Seward Peninsula, Alaska.* US Department of Interior, National Park Service, Anchorage, Alaska, Resources Report NPS/ARORCR/CRR-93/21.

Heiser, P. A., D. M. Hopkins, J. Brigham-Grette, S. Benson, V. F. Ivanov, and A. V. Lozhkin
1992 Pleistocene Glacial Geology of St. Lawrence Island, Alaska. *Geological Society of America Abstracts* 24:345.

Hoefle, C., M. E. Edwards, D. H. Mann, and V. Goetcheus
1994 Buried Soils and Vegetation on Seward Peninsula: A Window into the Paleoenvironment of the Bering Land Bridge - Current Status Report and Proposal. Report on file at National Park Service, Anchorage, Alaska, January 1994, 5 pp.

Hoefle, C., C. L. Ping, D.H. Mann, and M. E. Edwards
1994 Buried Soils on Seward Peninsula: A Window into the Paleoenvironment of the Bering Land Bridge. *Current Research in the Pleistocene* 11:134-136.

Hopkins, D. M.
1959 History of Imuruk Lake, Seward Peninsula, Alaska. *Geological Society of America Bulletin* 70:1033-1046.

1963 Geology of the Imuruk Lake area, Seward Peninsula, Alaska. *U.S. Geological Survey Bulletin* 1141-C, 100 pp.

1967 *The Bering Land Bridge* (ed.). Stanford University Press, Stanford.

1972 The paleogeography and climatic history of Beringia during late Cenozoic time. *Inter-Nord* 12:121-150.

1982 Aspects of the paleoecology of Beringia. In *Paleoecology of Beringia*, D. M. Hopkins, J. V.Matthews, C. E. Schweger, and S. B. Young (eds.). Academic Press, New York, pp 3-28.

1988 The Espenberg Maars: A record of Explosive Volcanic Activity in the Devil Mountain-Cape Espenberg Area, Seward Peninsula, Alaska. In *The Bering Land Bridge National Preserve: An Archeological Survey.* 2 volumes, U.S. Department of the Interior, National Park Service, Research/Resources Management Report No. AR-14, Anchorage.

Hopkins, D. M. and J. G. Kidd
1988 Thaw Lake Sediments and Sedimentary Environments. In *Permafrost, 5th International Conference Proceedings*, Trondheim, 1:790-795.

Hopkins, D. M., J. V. Matthews, C. E. Schweger and S. G. Young (eds.)
1982 *The Paleoecology of Beringia.* Academic Press, New York.

Hopkins, D. M., J. V. Matthews, J. A. Wolfe, and M. L. Silberman
1971 A Pliocene flora and insect fauna from the Bering Strait Region. *Paleogeography, Paleoclimatology, Paleoecology* 9:211-231.

Hopkins, D. M. and L. J. Plug
1994 Wetland and Thaw Lake Study, Bering Land Bridge National Preserve. Proposal submitted to National Park Service, Anchorage, Alaska, 9 pp.

Hopkins, D. M. and R. S. Sigafoos
1951 Frost Action and Vegetation Patterns on Seward Peninsula Alaska. *Geological Survey Bulletin* 974-C. U.S. Government Printing Office, Washington.

Jordan, J. W.
1988 Erosion characteristics and retreat rates along he north coast of Seward Peninsula. In *The Bering Land Bridge National Preserve: An Archeological Survey.* 2 volumes, U.S. Department of the Interior, National Park Service, Research/Resources Management Report No. AR-14, Anchorage, pp. 322-362.

1990 Late Holocene Development of Barrier Islands in the Southern Chukchi Sea, Alaska. Masters Thesis, University of Alaska Fairbanks, 1990.

Larsen, H.
1968 Trail Creek: Final Report on the Excavation of Two Caves on Seward Peninsula, Alaska. *Acta Arctica* Vol.15. Copenhagen.

Mason, O. K.
1988 The Sand Ridge Stratigraphy of northern Seward Peninsula. In *The Bering Land Bridge National Preserve: An Archeological Survey.* 2 volumes, U.S. Department of the Interior, National Park Service, Research/Resources Management Report No. AR-14, Anchorage, pp. 364-409.

1990 Beach Ridge Geomorphology of Kotzebue Sound: Implications for Paleoclimatology and Archaeology. Ph.D. Dissertation, Quaternary Science, University of Alaska, Fairbanks, 1990.

1992 A Geoarchaeological Methodology for Studying Prograding Coastal Sequences: Beach Ridge Geomorphology in Kotzebue Sound, Alaska. In *Paleoshorelines and Prehistory: An Exploration of Method*, L. L. Johnson and M. Strait (eds.), CRC Press, Boca Raton, pages 55-81.

1993 The Geoarchaeology of Beach Ridges and Cheniers: Studies of Coastal Evolution Using Archaeological Data. *Journal of Coastal Research* 9(1):126-146.

Mason, O. K. and J. W. Jordan
1991 A Proxy Late Holocene Climate Record Deduced from NW Alaska Beach Ridges. In *Proceedings, International Conference on the Role of Polar Regions in Global Change*, Volume II, G. Weller, C. Wilson, and B. Severin (eds.), Geophysical Institute, Fairbanks, pp. 649-657.

1993 Heightened North Pacific Storminess and Synchronous late Holocene Erosion of northwest Alaska Beach Ridge Complexes. *Quaternary Research* 40(1): 55-59.

Plug, L. J.
1993 Espenberg Wetlands Project: 1993 Field Report. Report on file at NPS Alaska System Support Office, Anchorage, 4 pp.

Powers, Wm. R., J. A. Adams, A. Godfrey, J. Ketz, D. Plaskett and G. R. Scott
1982 *The Chukchi-Imuruk Report: Archaeological Investigations in the Bering Land Bridge National Preserve, Seward Peninsula, Alaska, 1974 and 1975*. Cooperative Park Studies Unit, Occasional Paper No.31, University of Alaska, Fairbanks.

Schaaf, J. M.
1988 *The Bering Land Bridge National Preserve: An Archeological Survey*. 2 volumes, U.S. Department of the Interior, National Park Service, Research/Resources Management Report No. AR-14, Anchorage.

Simon, J. and S. C. Gerlach
1992 Reindeer Herding, Subsistence, and Alaskan Native Land Use in the Bering Land Bridge National Preserve Northern Seward Peninsula, Alaska: A Review of the Impact of Reindeer Herding on Community Relationships and Land Use in the Early Twentieth Century. Report on file at National Park Service, Anchorage, Alaska, 47 pp.

Vinson, D. M.
1988 Preliminary Report on Faunal Identifications from Trail Creek Caves. In *The Bering Land Bridge National Preserve: An Archeological Survey*. 2 volumes, U.S. Department of the Interior, National Park Service, Research/Resources Management Report No. AR-14, Anchorage, pp. 410-439.

1993 Taphonomic Analysis of Faunal Remains from Trail Creek Caves, Seward Peninsula, Alaska. Masters Thesis, University of Alaska Fairbanks, December 1993.

Danish archaeologist Helge Larsen at Trail Creek Caves, 1949.
~~ Photo by Charles Lucier, courtesy of the University of Alaska Anchorage archives.

Bessie (Elizabeth) Cross and Gideon Kahlook Barr Sr., 1939.
~~ Photo courtesy of Gideon Barr Sr. Photographer unknown.

David M. Hopkins in the Imuruk Lake area, on Hannum Creek a tributary of the Pinnell, then Inmachuk River, June 1948. ~~ Photo courtesy of D. M. Hopkins, taken by Jim Seitz.

~~ *We took this trip to examine and find the sources of the lava flows that form benches in the Inmachuk and Pinnell Rivers and Hannum Creek. We found a very large spring issuing from limestone, presumably from a cave on a hillside on the upper Inmachuk.*
~~ Dave Hopkins

Gideon Barr's Story about David Hopkins at Work in Northwest Alaska, 1966

*Here, there were two white men surveying the land.
Dave Hopkins spent two summers land surveying.
He would come the first part of July.*

*When he first came, I took him boating
    when he was collecting samples.
I boated him with my small boat.
He would survey below us and collect samples
    from the bottom.
He used a shovel-like implement to collect samples.
This was dragged using a long rope.*

*When we used an outboard motor, the shovel
    would fill up right away.
Then when it was full,
We would start from the shallows near the beach line.
Then [we would] go out about five miles.*

*The rope was not five miles long.
I estimated it to be about three miles long.
We would drag it until it got full.
Hopkins wrote everything down and then
    saved the samples, too.
It was just like hunting for sunk ugruk.
We would drag the line as if we were hooking for ugruk.*

*When the shovel was being emptied, I say to him:
    When I look over the land, above us—
    The distance is equal to open water in the winter—
    When you sink an ugruk and hook for it,
    when we are hooking.
    We hook starfish from this area.
The distance [then] would be about here from the land.*

West shore of Lava Lake. From left, Bob Sigafoos, botanist; Wilbur Quay, cook and mammologist; Inmachuk, a yellow sled dog loaned to Hopkins by Fred Rohn of Nome; and David Hopkins, August 1948.
~ Photo courtesy of David Hopkins. Photo by Jim Seitz or Art Fernald.

The Cold War had begun and our assignment was to "study permafrost" and to evaluate the possibility of "building an airstrip on the lava beds. A near hurricane had nearly knocked our tents down and our clothes and bedding were all soaked, and we were taking a day off to dry out and catch up on our notes. Sigafoos, Fernald, and Quay were recruited by me and were fellow students at Harvard. I hired Bill Quay because he was a student of mammology. He set small traps and deadfalls all around our camps, caught voles, and shrews, and spent evenings skinning out the little carcasses while the rest of us played bridge. We rarely ate earlier than 9:00 and joked about the probable rodent origin of the meat in our meals.

~ David Hopkins

August 1948 camp at the west end of Kuzitrin Lake. Probably Bob Sigafoos standing between the tents. The white tents were standard US Geological Survey 8' x 10' floored sailcloth sleeping tents. The three small brown tents were early backpacking tents called "mountain tents." ~~ Photo by David Hopkins.

The shovel did not scoop any starfish.
The one that empties and has a screen on top.
It does not take most of the sand, which just seeps through.
Only the longer ones are taken, the ones
    that are too large for the screen.

He looked at me.
We were dragging the scoop.
He says this is the last time we are dragging it.
Then it is being dragged.
When it filled up, we stopped and he took pictures.
Then he took a compass and shoots toward the east,
    toward the bluff.
He would take more pictures.
He would obtain the degrees from the compass,
    then write them down.

Then, he pulled the scoop.
Included in the scoop were live starfish.
He says to me:
    … The Inupiat know what the ocean bottom has.
     They study it, too.
The Inupiat are very observant when they are hunting.
He said my words were accurate.
The scoop had picked up live starfish.

I said—I know this area.
I know even the ocean depth.
The land—same way.
I said I have been seeing this, and understand it.
Hunting to fulfill our appetite and to fill our stomachs—
With that in mind, we search for food.
We have to do it.

He said that I am right.
When I say there was a flood according
    to the Bible, the land was flooded.
He says that I am right.
Also, at Kialiik and Serpentine Hot Springs hills,

Bering Land Bridge - Early Research -- 29

Charles Lucier (left), Taylor Moto (center), and Helge Larsen examine a recent textile found in a cave at Trail Creek Caves, 1949-1950.
~~ Photo courtesy of University of Alaska archives. Photographer unknown.

A young Zaccheus William "Bill" Barr, Gideon's younger brother and unidentified person at Trail Creek Caves, 1949-1950. Bill was camphand for the archaeological excavations. ~~ Photo by Charles Lucier.

*Our fathers always say there are beach sea shells
    to the west of the hills.
The water line is noticeable because wood chips,
    pieces of small beach-wood,
    are laying side by side on top where the rocks
    are located.
It is easy to see this by looking at the lopsided rocks
    leaning in the same direction.
I told him this as well.*

*This area has a lot of seashells on the tip of Devil Mountain.
Toward the west—on the steepest slopes.
Because my papa (Makaiqtaq) would say that
    when he was a boy.
After seeing it [the seashells] for the first time,
    he said, "Holy Cow!"
He said the biblical account of the flood is correct,
    certainly true.
Up at Kialiik, the water line is visible.
Seashells are abundant there too.*

*My father saw this when they were new
    and when he was young too.
He followed the ones who walked and had always followed
    them ever since.
When he walked [in those days], his memory was keen.
When he looked around he saw seashells and wood bark,
    wood piles and tree bark.
But they had shrunk.
Only the wood was in good shape.
It is certainly true when the earth flooded...*

*In July, Dave Hopkins came.
When he first came up to this area, he went up to dig.
To the hills called Qilugitiknik.
The bottom of the hills are flat tundra.
These are the only hills here.
Then he told us that the permafrost is too close.
What he shoveled out is real interesting.*

Making camp in August 1961 on the east shore of Kotzebue Sound, west shore of Baldwin Peninsula, about five miles southwest of Cape Blossom. Dave McCulloch bending over, Dan Lisburne lighting stove, Dick Janda hidden behind Dan's left shoulder, Willie Goodwin, Jr. in black with back to camera.
~ Photo by David Hopkins.

Launching the skinboat. Dan Lisburne pulling the prow, Dick Janda on the right side of the boat, Willy Goodwin Jr. picking up a piece of driftwood, and Dave Hopkins pushing the stern, August 1961. The boat is rolling on an inflated seal skin.
~~ Photo courtesy of Dave Hopkins. Photo by Dave McCulloch.

In 1961, with two excellent assistants, I decided it was time to examine the cliffs of the Baldwin Peninsula, where Hershey 40 years earlier had reported glacial till -- a seeming impossibility so far from the mountains. So we flew to Kotzebue where I met Dan Lisburne who was in town to buy supplies to take back to Point Hope.

This was a wonderful trip. We spent nights telling each other stories around the campfire. Dan attempted to teach us Inupiaq, starting with the obscenities. Dan's boat was made of two ugruk skins. Dan, then about 35, was born near Cape Lisburne and attended the BIA high school at Eklutna. He said he liked to go travelling along new stretches of the coast and (for a modest price) would be glad to take us down the Baldwin Peninsula, which he had never seen. He wanted a boatman, and proposed that we hire the son of Willy Goodwin, who worked for Bullock and Rotman's lightering and fuel service.

In later years, Dan was on the city council of Point Hope and was a leader among the Point Hope people who began to resist the use of an atomic bomb to excavate a harbor on what they considered their land at Ogotoruk Creek. Still later, he spent at least one term in the legislature. Willy Goodwin Jr. was very young -- maybe still in high school. He wore his hair very long, which provoked jokes from Dan. In the 1980s, Willy was a powerful figure in Kotzebue. Dick Janda was a graduate student at Berkeley with my oldest and best friend, Clyde Wahrhaftig. Dick was an excellent geologist and spent the last part of his career studying Mt. St. Helens. ~~ Dave Hopkins

---

He thought it was real interesting when they came back.
He planned to return in September of the next year
*   and dig before freeze-up.*
They would dig before the ground freezes.

For sure, the next September he came around
*   and continued his digging.*
He went to Espenberg by plane.
Then he went by boat, stopping when we got close
*   to the hills.*
From there, we went by foot to the hills.
When they went up the first time,
*   they say it was real interesting.*
They did not say what they meant by "real interesting."
They spoke, however, about how Eskimos had used this area
*   and if they knew the history.*
Here, I told them about my father Thomas Makaiqtaq
*   who told a story that the ground in this area*
*   was once floating.*
That was before his time.

The land had just formed.
It was forming at that time, he would say.
The [researchers] would have a big grin [about this]
*   without saying a thing.*
Somehow, they were understanding.
When I told the story right, they would say
*   it was real interesting...*
At first, when I told them the story, I did not tell them
*   the real meaning of the story.*

The following year they were gone for a long time—
*   from one week to ten days.*
They spent about that much time up there [in the hills].
When they came back, dirt had accumulated
*   all over their bodies.*
They were digging all that time, and digging
*   at the pond edges, too.*
They were going in a westerly direction.

Trail Creek Caves in the Bering Land Bridge National Preserve. ~ Photo by Jeanne Schaaf.

Prehistoric hunters were known to have used the interior regions seasonally for at least the past 9,000 years, based on Helge Larsen's excavations at Trail Creek Caves in 1949 and 1950 (Larsen 1968). Located at the northern periphery of the Imuruk lava plateau in limestone and marble uplands, these caves yielded hunting implements dating to about 9,000 years ago and from about 5,000 years ago to recent times. This site is located along a trail to the interior hunting grounds of the Goodhope River and Imuruk Lake areas, a trail still used by hunters from Deering, located on the southern coast of Kotzebue Sound. ~ Jeanne Schaaf

James Louis Giddings (left) and Dave McCulloch, Cape Krusenstern old whaling site, July 1961. ~ Photo by Dave Hopkins.

On this day, Louis Giddings walked us through the whole 40-odd beach ridge sequence of Cape Krusenstern. Late in the day and still a couple of miles from camp, I finally gave in and asked Louis, "Couldn't we walk a little slower? I'm beat!" Louis replied, "I was just about to ask you that. You're a geologist, and I thought you were setting the pace!" Note the antique "Trapper Nelson" backpack, which you HAD to wear if you wanted to be a real Alaskan and a prospective sourdough! ~ Dave Hopkins

*Dave Hopkins was telling stories this time.
He said the water line was up there at one time.
Seashells and clam shells are layered [over each other]
　　slightly slanted:
　　　"The shoreline was up there at one time."
I was absolutely correct when I told him these stories.
The stories I told were true.*

*Inupiat have history, too.
History passed on by telling stories.
Our stories, they say, are absolutely true.*

*It is true that the water extended all the way up
　　to those hills.
They say the water turned into land not too long ago.
The ground had floated for thousands and thousands of years.
The ground had ice only on the top portion,
　　covered by a thin layer of ice.
They were saying that and understood it that way
　　when they dug.
The seashells are found in layers—all the way
　　to the permafrost or floor.
They would mark a line every time they found something.
Because the seashells in layers become older
　　when you go down deeper.
[They know this] from when they dug with their shovels,
　　from what they dug up.*

It is a proof that our stories are true.

*When Dave Hopkins was looking for things from the ground...
The last time I worked with him was at Cape Blossom,
　　across from Kigasruanalui...
The last time I worked with him was from Sinik
　　all the way down to Ikpik.*

*He also checked the lagoon floor to see how it was made,
　　after he completed the ocean side.
Also, he surveyed Wales Lagoon, but it had nothing.*

Bush pilot John Milton Cross (left) and with his wife, Bessie Barr Cross, and their children, Mary Sue (Anderson), Dallas, and Milton in Kotzebue, 1956 or 1957 (right). ~ Photos by Howard E. Jackson, courtesy of Mary Sue (Cross) Anderson.

Portrait of Bessie Barr Cross fishing for tomcod in Kotzebue Sound, 1952 or 1953. Bessie recalled, "I had just had my hair permed and wanted to show it off, but the photographer made me cover it up because Eskimos weren't supposed to have curly hair!" ~~ Photo by Frank H. Whaley taken for Wien Air Service, courtesy of Mary Sue (Cross) Anderson.

He did not study that too much.
It seems like he ran out of funding.
Congress, perhaps, did not appropriate money...
The pay (for this research) originated from Washington, D. C.
This must be true, because he stopped studying.
But maybe he went to another place to do more studies.
He wanted to study the Russian land too.
He said he had worked in six continents...

The last time he worked, his assistant was a Russian.
We were dragging a long rope and the ground caved in.
The ground had layers and layers that were visible to interpret.
The hills on the shoreline [of the Tapqaq coast]
  are not too many—only in a few areas.
The flooding has washed them away and [there have been]
  some cave-ins.
That's how it is at Cape Blossom.
A lot of the hills are caved-in, and they also studied these.

These hills were not drifted.
They were upright before, and they had fallen.
When one fell, our partner measured it from above,
  downward.
Then he would write it down.
He would analyze it with the microscope and then work
  on them down below [in the lower '48] during the winter...
They had collected samples to study the history.
This work involves a lot of studying, trying to interpret things.
They would learn [from this] what had happened
  so many years ago by studying the samples.
Also, Dave Hopkins went across to Russia to study their land.
He did not know the words of the Bible, including the part
  about the big flood.
[The water] must have split through the narrow part at Wales.
They would talk about this.

... Elephant bones and teeth are found [in this area]
  along with the hair.
They also found one that must have been whole and intact.

"Your Man in Yakutia," August 1969. Dave Hopkins on an International Quaternary Association field trip in northeast Siberia. This segment of the trip was along the road from Bestyakh and Amga. ~~ Photo courtesy of David Hopkins. Russian photographer unidentified.

Dave Hopkins, his daughter Chindi, examining stratigraphy along the Espenberg River, 1970. ~ Photo courtesy of David Hopkins. Photographer unknown.

Ground sliding had exposed the animal.
It might still be there unless a mud slide has covered it.
The land slides only when it is raining hard.
The elephant had hair and must be whole.
But [these scientists] never went back to it.

It is known that these animals crossed when they were alive
   and when there was land all the way across.
This is certainly believable.
It was like that before—animals were crossing from Russia.
In their land, the animals were the same like ours.
They were the same.
They never swam when they went across, these big animals.
These wild animals had traveled through land
   since time immemorial.

The land they had used for crossing was not very wide.
A big flood must have split it up.
When they talked about this, [the scientists] would go
   into an argument.
Either one was trying to win.
The other one [the Russian scientist] did not speak English too
   well, even though he understood it.
He could not pronounce some of the words.

[This argument happened] while we were having dinner.
Their plane air dropped us steaks and vegetables.
It was real windy and we were storm bound
   at the end of Kuugaasiaq.
When we were making dinner, we opened a can
   of corn-on-the-cob.
There were four of us: my son, Dave Hopkins, the Russian,
   and myself.
The Russian, after eating steak, he picked up a whole corn.
After picking it up, he said "uusruuski..."
He said that this is how they are called in Russian...
This is just like we speak in Inupiaq too.
The way we pronounce words are understandable.
Some of their sayings are similar to Inupiaq words...

~~ *I value Gideon as a true scholar devoted to the preservation and transmission of oral traditions that he first learned during his childhood; devoted to conserving -- by doing -- skills such as seal-netting under the winter ice; and devoted, finally, to the lovely landscape in which he has always lived.* ~~

~~ David Hopkins

Gideon Kahlook Barr Sr., August 1993.
~~ Photo by James Magdanz.

Charlie Lucier (left) and Dave Hopkins meet at Trail Creek Caves in July 1995 for the first time since their initial meeting there in 1949. ~ Photo by Jeanne Schaaf.

> *and he was a good interpreter.*
>
> *In their heated argument, one [scholar] would try to win.*
> *It seemed like they would start fighting physically at any time.*
> *The Russian had handwriting that could not be understood,*
>   *and he would present what he had been writing too.*
> *They would argue over their writings, saying one was wrong*
>   *while the other is right...*
> *Because the two worked together, they taught each other*
>   *their respective languages.*
> *They were doing good work.*
>
> *Here, my story ends again.*
>   ~ Gideon K. Barr Sr., 1983

John Cross, an old bush pilot I worshiped, had some things he wanted to show me. Among them were the caves at Trail Creek where some Inupiaq men from Deering and Candle had gotten weathered-in during a blizzard. John said, "Being miners, they had some dynamite with them and thought it would be prudent to toss some dynamite into the cave before they entered it." Out came a bear, then another, and then a third! At that time I was a little bit green to Alaska, and it didn't seem peculiar to me that there were three bears in a cave.

So we planned the next year, which was 1948, to make a long backpacking trip down Cottonwood Creek to Trail Creek. In Nome we bought a lot of fireworks, some Roman candles and sky rockets; and we also bought a small amount of lumber so we could make a launching chute. So we had nails, of course, and we had our geology picks. So we came down here to the creek mouth, a gorge choked with willows below the caves. I must say my heart was palpitating as we made our way up the creek through the willows, knowing how many bears were likely to be in this valley. Opposite what we now know as Cave 2, we built our little rocket launcher. We attempted to launch the sky rockets. They hit the cliff near the cave. Then we got out the Roman candles, and we managed to get a couple of those into the cave. And the three bears didn't come out. So I was the fearless leader, and we went on our hands and knees into the cave. What I remember was a knife in my teeth, a 30-06 in one hand, and a flashlight in the other. And we went all the way back into the cave. Didn't see a single bear.
                             ~ David Hopkins.

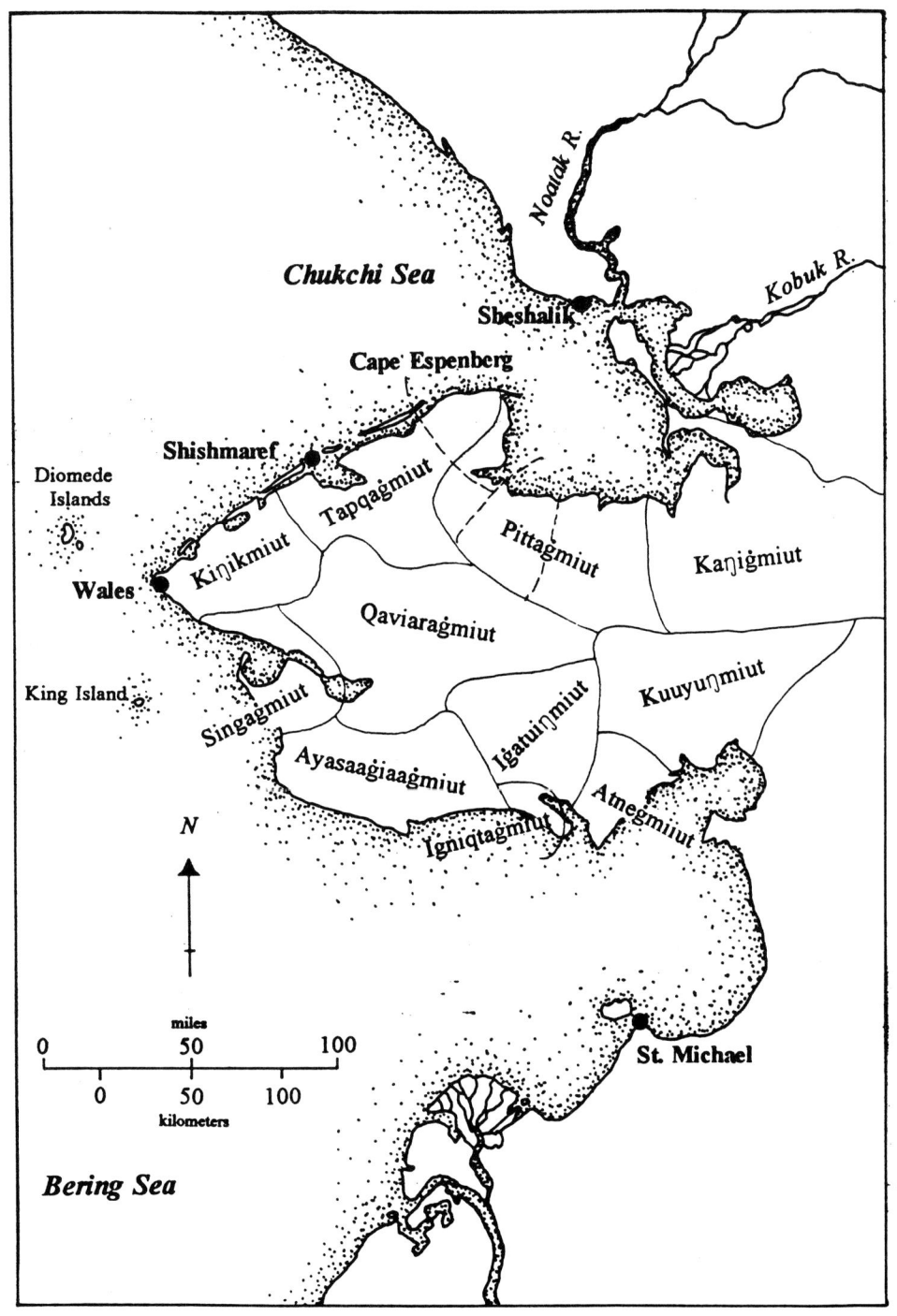

Before Our Fathers' Time

Late Prehistoric Inupiat of the Northern Seward Peninsula

(Opposite)
Nineteenth century Inupiaq and Yupik territories, Seward Peninsula (adapted from Burch 1994 and Ray 1984). Dashed lines are Ray's Espenberg and Goodhope territories.
~~ Map from Schaaf 1995.

After the land bridge connection was severed about 9,500 years ago, cultural and biological exchanges between the Old and New Worlds continued, just as climate and environments continued to change. By 2,000 years ago the Bering Strait area was less a gateway, as monikers such as "bridge" and "crossroads" suggest, than a well-established culture center thought to be comprised of distinct cultural groups settled in large permanent villages with highly developed marine-based technologies, elaborate art, and extensive trade networks (cf. Arutiunov and Fitzhugh 1988:117-129).

By the early 1800s, six to seven Inupiaq and four Yupik societies are thought to have inhabited the Seward Peninsula (Burch 1980, 1994; Ray 1984). These 19th-century societies were characterized by 1) a distinct group name, 2) an ideology of distinctiveness, 3) a discrete territory, 4) a distinct dialect or subdialect, 5) a high level of endogamy (marriage within one's own group), 6) a distinct seasonal round, and 7) a material culture that was distinct in some detail of structure or ornamentation (Burch 1988:4). Although the existence of separate dialects and subdialects suggests stable development in the area for a long time, it is unknown how long these traditional societies had existed before their demise, which began in the late 1830s and was complete by the end of the nineteenth century (Burch 1980:279, 282). Anthropologists have postulated the existence of these societies based on reconstructed ethnographies (ethnographies constructed from the oral traditions remembered by people born after 1860). These societies have never been materially demonstrated in the archaeological record, but if this could be done, questions about the development and stability of these societies could be addressed. The archaeological record holds the key to answering questions about when these social systems may have appeared and why and how they developed.

I set out to examine the existing archaeological database for material culture patterns that may provide insight into the social and economic organization of the late-prehistoric Inupiat (circa AD 1500-1800) on the northern Seward Peninsula within what is now the Bering Land Bridge National Preserve. One purpose of the study was to discover if patterns identified in the late-prehistoric archaeological record corresponded with the proposed territories of the distinct nineteenth-century Inupiaq societies.

To address these questions, I evaluated the known archaeological record, consisting largely of survey data, and chose to focus on two characteristics attributed to the nineteenth-century societies: evidence of discrete territories and material culture differences -- postulated in my study to be manifested by distinct house types.

The archaeological data base is well-suited to this study because it is dominated by late-prehistoric winter settlements, with 493 mapped semi-subterranean house depressions distributed across the 17,500 square-kilometer (10,850 square-mile) study area. The 19th-century Inupiat societies maintained territories centered on the drainage systems of major rivers; and during winter when warfare and raiding were common, virtually all of a society's members could be found within their own territory at settlements located near the core of the territory relative to fishing inland and sealing at the coast (Burch 1988:10). Therefore, I divided the study area into four major drainage units to examine the data sets for patterns in the distribution of late-prehistoric winter settlements and distinct house types for comparison with the patterns described for the nineteenth-century Inupiat.

This study was focused on the archaeological record primarily in the Tapqagmiut, Qaviaragmiut, and Pittagmiut territories and in the region of Kuzitrin and Imuruk Lakes, where the Qaviaragmiut,

Pittagmiut, Fish River, and Koyuk River territories met. The Pittagmiut are the least known among the Inupiaq societies of Northwest Alaska (Burch 1994:391), but this is also the area that is best documented archaeologically and is the home territory of my primary informant Gideon Kahlook Barr Sr. (born 1917), his parents Thomas Makaiqtaq (born ca. 1869) and Emily Paizuzraq Kiyutelluk Barr (born 1897), his paternal grandparents Kunautaq and Kuvaaq, and his maternal grandparents.

The Kuzitrin and Imuruk Lake area is particularly interesting because the proposed nineteenth-century territorial boundaries converged in a very rich resource area, evidenced by fishing and small- to large-scale caribou-hunting sites dating from as early as 4,500 years ago to within the last few hundred years. Oral historical records indicate that boundaries were both commonly trespassed and aggressively defended there.

A series of atypical sites, unique in the arctic archaeological record, is located along this convergence of historic boundaries. These sites are substantial villages with as many as 25 houses, exceptionally large in a region where villages of seven or more houses are considered large, associated with massive stone monuments, and situated atop ancient volcanic cinder cones and lava complexes. The importance of the landforms and cultural features for caribou-procurement and meat-storage is apparent; but the concentrations of winter houses on lookout promontories, without readily available water and fuel and in addition, associated with monumental architectural features, are unexplained. It is possible that they represent a response to boundary perturbations related to population movements or to changes in resource availability due to climatic change. It is also possible that they represent occupation of a strategic area important for controlling a key resource (caribou) or the flow of Native and European trade goods in the eighteenth century. My findings, which are excerpted from a separate independent study (Schaaf 1995) are discussed and summarized below.

The focused study of the distribution of house types classified from survey data and a regional comparison of the house types suggests the presence of distinct material culture traditions dictating house form in the late-prehistoric period. There is a very marked distinction between the house forms used along the Chukchi Sea coast from Cape Espenberg west to the Bering Strait and the houses built along the shore of Kotzebue Sound and in the inland portions of the study area (Imuruk Lake and Kuzitrin River areas). This patterning, which appears to have been consistent throughout the examined late-prehistoric record in the study area, must have been created by the long-term repetitive ways in that people positioned themselves on the landscape. In addition, a marked discontinuity in the settlement pattern in the Imuruk lava plateau area suggests that the processes producing the patterns were disturbed.

The earliest large villages in the study area are located at Cape Espenberg, where they coincide temporally with the Late Western Thule period (AD 1250-1400) as defined at Cape Krusenstern (Giddings and Anderson 1986). However, at Cape Krusenstern we also see a disturbance in the pattern of house types. Before AD 1400, houses at Cape Krusenstern are like those used at Cape Espenberg, with a slight localized variation regarding the placement of the kitchens. After AD 1400, houses associated with the Kobuk River appear at Cape Krusenstern and seem to replace the earlier house types (Giddings and Anderson 1986). A similar displacement is not seen at Cape Espenberg in the late-prehistoric record.

The study also revealed a pronounced homogeneity in the occurrence of house types within the drainage units and within sites. Recognizing that both environmental and cultural parameters influence house form, this pattern in the distribution of house types is interpreted as reflecting some degree of material culture differences among the people occupying the northern Seward Peninsula Chukchi Sea coast and those occupying the shore of Kotzebue Sound and the inland areas.

Based on house type, the archaeological sites from Cowpack Lagoon (Kuukpak) to Cape Espenberg are most closely aligned with the Bering Strait area. Houses with long entryways (greater than or equal to four meters [13.2 feet]) and storm sheds, some with one or more side rooms attached to the passageway, dominate in late-prehistoric sites along the coast from Espenberg southwest to Ikpik (Schaaf 1988). The distribution of these house types appears to correspond with the nineteenth-century territories as outlined by Ray (1984:286), rather than with the Pittagmiut territory as delineated by Burch (1994:4).

While the archaeological data at Cape Espenberg show a continuity in house form and settlement pattern from the fourteenth century to the nineteenth century (and perhaps as early as the seventh century AD), oral historical and historical census data indicate that early in the nineteenth-century occupation of this area was in a state of change resulting in depopulation of the area or perhaps movement into the area by a people called the Malimiut (or Malemiut, a Yupik word used on Norton Sound that refers to Inupiaq dialect speakers from Northwest Alaska) from the Kobuk and Selawik River areas (Ray 1967). Burch postulates that Cape Espenberg was occupied by Malimiut speakers by the early 1800s (1994).

Existing data from the study area do not indicate a decrease in settlement size from early to late-prehistoric times (AD 1250 to 1800) or the disappearance of large villages by historic times as was found in the Kobuk River area (Giddings 1952:112) and the Cape Krusenstern area (Giddings and Anderson 1986). Giddings also noted a trend toward standardization of house form by the middle of the eighteenth century, abandonment of deep, permanent winter homes, and disappearance of the use of passageways or tunnels by recent times. Except for the early-historic disappearance of passageways, these trends are not apparent in the Seward Peninsula study area. Giddings postulated that some of the changes along the Kobuk River were related to increased nomadism and the effects of large-scale use of dog traction after AD 1700. Excavation data are needed to determine actual village size of large settlements recorded in the study area; however, surface indications and site layout in some cases suggest that in some of the large villages, the houses were constructed at the same time and used for perhaps several decades. Dog traction, rather than encouraging nomadism, seems to have allowed the late-prehistoric Inupiat to maintain large winter villages at good fishing sites, supported by the retrieval of large inland caches of dried caribou meat procured during the previous summer.

In organizational terms, it is important to note an interesting difference between food storage and risk-sharing strategies of the settlements in the inland (Imuruk Lake and Kuzitrin River) and Kotzebue Sound areas versus the settlements on the Chukchi Sea coast. The large clusters of stone caches in the Imuruk Lake area appear to represent a community risk-sharing strategy, exemplified by the nineteenth-century communal caribou hunts and subsequent mass storage of meat conducted by the Qaviaragmiut and the Pittagmiut. The late Jack Ningeulook from Shishmaref said that the long entryways characteristic of the houses used along the Chukchi Sea coast were necessary to protect individual family food stores from pilfering by others in the community during food shortages. This indicates reliance on a household strategy rather than a community strategy to deal with winter survival. This suggestion is supported by the distribution of small cache pits around individual late-prehistoric houses and the lack of large clusters of caches along the northern Chukchi coast. The upshot is that this implies social organizational differences that correspond to the pattern of house type distribution.

The occupation of large settlements in the study area from the fourteenth to the nineteenth centuries coincides with the Little Ice Age (LIA), a period of generally cooler climate marked by glacier advances in Alaska (Grove 1988; Calkin and Wiles 1990). More importantly, the LIA was characterized by drastic weather variability - lower lows and higher highs. These irregularities would have required immediate social and economic responses, especially if sea-ice and snow-cover conditions or the timing of freezeup and breakup were to change, thereby changing the availability of key early spring and fall resources. Glacial evidence in the Kigluaik Mountains on the southern Seward Peninsula indicates that a major, maximum high temperature occurred in the early to mid-1700s. This corresponds roughly with a dramatic increase in the number of interior tundra sites in north Alaska (cf. Anderson 1984:92) and also is coincidental with the large-scale use of dog traction in place by AD 1700 (Giddings 1952:112).

Few data about the actual effects of the LIA on terrestrial and marine resources exist, and researchers disagree about whether the effects were less severe inland than on the coast (Mason and Gerlach 1995:113-115). For the Seward Peninsula, where the Inupiat depended on both coastal and inland resources, whether obtained from within their own territories or through intergroup alliances, this may be a moot point. Certainly the regional and local effects of the LIA were complex, and adverse conditions in one area may have resulted in resource enhancement in another.

Elsewhere in Alaska, cultural responses to the effects of the LIA are reflected by sudden and widespread shifts in settlement patterns beginning around AD 1400. On Kodiak Island, for example, there was a shift away from sea-mammal hunting to fishing, a dramatic increase in village and house size (multiple-roomed houses), and an increase in conflict and warfare (Knecht 1995).

The archaeological evidence examined in the Seward Peninsula study area, indicates that the large villages situated atop volcanic cinder cones in the Kuzitrin/Imuruk Lakes area are single-component and were occupied for a brief period of time, possibly only a few seasons. Site use may have continued for meat storage or as caribou lookout stations, after the habitations were abandoned. Although present data are insufficient to securely date the time of occupation, these sites are thought to predate the mid-nineteenth century.

Above- and below-ground stone caches and alignments or caribou-drive lines (inuksuit) are scattered in this same area on high ground and lava flows. These fit well with the nineteenth-century Pittagmiut and Qaviaragmiut pattern of inland late-summer caribou drives at lakes, where meat was dried and stored for retrieval by dog sled after freezeup. William Oquilluk recounts that a few hunters would stay up to a month after a successful drive while the meat was drying (1981:97-99). Winter villages in the area, however, are anomalous. LIA-induced changes in resource abundances and distribution may have led to different subsistence emphases. Yet given the mobility at the time, winter settlements would have been located along water bodies or rivers to maximize access to other resources. On the cinder cones, there was only one primary resource, caribou, and a migratory one at that. Additionally, Burch's (1988:9-10) sources never associated the location of nineteenth-century freezeup sites with caribou procurement.

Could these out-of-place winter villages reflect the interactions of distinct societies? The nineteenth-century Inupiaq and Yupik territory boundaries were generally in resource-poor areas (Burch 1980:276), and yet these boundaries were "sharply defined" and "jealously guarded" (Ray 1967:381). In the Kuzitrin and Imuruk Lake area, where the cinder-cone villages occurred, four territory boundaries converged in a very rich resource area, especially important to the Pittagmiut, the Qaviaragmiut, and their allies. Ray states that the Koyuk River people "aggressively coveted" the Kuzitrin Lake area, which was likewise aggressively defended by the Qaviaragmiut as the lake was the headwaters of the Kuzitrin River and an extremely important place for fish and caribou procurement (1967:383).

The late-prehistoric villages atop the cinder cones and the extensive complexes of caribou-drive lines, hunting blinds, meat caches, and monumental architecture are located along the Continental Divide, separating the drainages defining the territories of four nineteenth-century societies. Twin Calderas most certainly played a key role in large-scale caribou procurement, yet the massive stone monuments there are more elaborate than required to encourage directional movements of caribou. In other regions monuments have been interpreted as geographical symbols erected by local competing groups and which may have been more important in times of economic stress and related conflict (Hodder 1979:450).

The tall well-built cairns at Gosling Cone, Skeleton, Butte, Twin Cairns, Rocky Point, Cygnus Cone, Cassiope Cone, and Virginia Butte, among others, all along the Continental Divide in the Imuruk Lake area, may therefore have been territorial symbols. They would have clearly marked ownership of resources and territory in a lowland area where drainage divides were not obvious. Here the drainages disappear into vast wetlands that drain in two or more directions, therefore if territories were divided according to drainages, there may have been a need to clearly mark boundaries in this area.

The defensive locations of the cinder-cone villages present a second line of evidence that suggests the villages arose during conflict. Occupants of the cinder-cone summits would have had the distinct advantage in bow-and-arrow battles with intruders approaching from the surrounding lowlands. This pattern of defensive occupations is seen elsewhere in Alaska during the late-prehistoric period. In the Gulf of Alaska and Southeast Alaska, there was a rise during late-prehistoric times in the use of refuge rocks, sheer-walled headlands, or islands (Knecht 1995; Moss and Erlandson 1992). By the eighteenth century, the Northwest Coast saw widespread population movements, destabilization of traditional boundaries, and prevalent warfare, with a proliferation of small forts along travel routes to control the flow of valuable European trade goods (Ferguson, 1983; MacDonald 1984, 1989).

An alignment of large oval depressions strung along the northeast edge of Skeleton Butte, a cinder cone supporting a village with 25 winter houses, may have been entrenchments. They are not cache or house depressions and their purpose remains unknown. Three other features at Skeleton Butte are large, deep rock-walled structures located at the south end of the village and near the west edge of the butte. These features were called "fortifications" by Deering people. After brief examination of these features, this explanation seems unlikely. The cavities of these structures are at least two meters (6.6 feet) deep and up to four meters (13.2 feet) in interior diameter. They have no openings in the wall and from inside the structures there is no tactical advantage. Furthermore, the position of the structures does not appear to correspond with defense of a likely avenue of attack (from the south or the east). I think that they are more likely to have been massive storage structures, perhaps reflecting a practice akin to the strategy of storing immense quantities of food in the fortified village of Kitwanga in British Columbia (MacDonald 1984:70).

If the large villages and stone monuments along the Continental Divide are indicative of conflict, what might have precipitated and intensified the conflict to the degree that settlement patterns were disrupted and villages were established on the cinder cones?

In the 1800s, warfare between traditional societies in Northwest Alaska was sophisticated, widespread, and intense (Burch 1974). Generally, raids were surprise attacks on villages, carried out on foot after dark, most often in winter after the ground was frozen but before heavy snowfall. A large war party could attack in the open in any season. In open battles, the uphill, upwind position was superior (Burch 1974:10). The location of the cinder-cone villages suggests a heightened state of war readiness beyond the general state of watchfulness for sporadic raiders from more typical settlement locations.

LIA climatic fluctuations could have had serious effects on both inland and coastal resources, as discussed earlier. If, for example, sea-mammal hunting were greatly curtailed, as researchers have shown for both Kotzebue Sound (Giddings and Anderson 1986) and the Gulf of Alaska (Knecht 1995), greater pressure would be placed on caribou and other inland resources. Already probably an area of conflict over abundant resources, the need to defend access to critical resources in the Iumuruk-Kuzitrin Lake area would have been intensified by LIA-induced changes in resource availability.

Consideration of other factors influencing inter-societal conflict for the control of resources must include late-prehistoric Native trade. The importance of pre-contact Native trade between societies in Northwest Alaska and across the Bering Strait has been underscored by several researchers (Burch and Correll 1972; Burch 1984, 1988a; Foote 1965; Hickey 1979; Ray 1967, 1975). This far-reaching trade system was

> a highly organized massive effort involving thousands of human beings every year, some of whom invested considerable amounts of human energy and capital into resource harvesting, manufacturing, and transportation of surplus goods. It was a network with rules of its own, transcending local social conventions, and may have helped to bind a number of autonomous societies into an apparent whole....
>
> (Hickey 1979:420)

From the earliest European accounts about the Bering Strait area we know that by the beginning of the eighteenth century, the Seward Peninsula Inupiat actively interacted through trade and warfare with the Chukchi. Tobacco, beads, and iron items, especially iron lances, were highly desired by the Alaska Natives in exchange for furs and ready-made clothing, such as vests of young caribou and rabbit skins (Kotzebue 1821:I:205,229; Ray 1975:49).

Maintaining the structure of this trade network and control of the flow of goods, especially European goods, which were scarce through the eighteenth century, was extremely important, as demonstrated by the 1836 attack on St. Michael, a Russian post established three years earlier in Norton Sound. The Seward Peninsula Inupiat, probably the Qaviaragmiut, Sledge Islanders, and King Islanders, had established a trade route south from the Bering Strait to the Yukon River (Ray 1975:125). The Russian post intercepted this trade and disrupted the established Native trade network, bringing on a bow-and-arrow attack, which the Russians lost.

Caribou skins and fawn skins were among the most common, though not the most valuable, trade items offered by the Northwest Alaska Natives (Foote 1965:118; Ray 1975:125). The archaeological and oral historical data examined in this study have demonstrated the historic and prehistoric focus on caribou procurement in the Imuruk-Kuzitrin Lake area. It is possible that the cinder-cone villages and monuments were established to protect boundaries and access to a critical resource in a time of accelerated trade beginning with the Anyui-Kolyma trade fair initiated in 1789. Ray's research shows that Malimiut-dialect speakers began moving south and west onto the Seward Peninsula in the late 1700s when they became middlemen in the Russian-Native trade market (Ray 1967;390). They undoubtedly moved onto the Seward Peninsula to gain control of an important Native fur-trade route from the Yukon to the Buckland River and Kotzebue Sound (cf. Foote 1965:112; Ray 1975:129), as well as control of key points in Norton Sound.

In response to the intrusive population movement, resident groups may have taken measures to protect access to resources and perhaps to control trade and travel routes, resulting in the establishment of the "outpost" villages on the cinder cones observed in the archaeological record. The increased trade may have increased demand and therefore led to greater resource stress and scarcity, in turn resulting in greater conflict.

The cinder-cone sites are probably related to protection and control of access to caribou and perhaps large supplies of cached meat for the people occupying the Qaviaragmiut and probably the eastern portion of the Pittagmiut territories (as defined by Burch 1994) in late prehistoric times. Conflict for this resource in an area that was possibly a calving ground may have been due to climatic pressures, increased demand due to accelerated trade, or even perhaps due to conflict over accumulated food (Ferguson 1983). If the actual time of occupation of these sites is the late 1700s, their use may have been short term due to the rapid disruption of Native trade networks by American traders and whalers beginning in the 1840s.

The archaeological survey and testing data compiled and analyzed in this study do suggest the presence of distinct late-prehistoric groups. Distribution of house forms appears to reflect separate and long-standing cultural differences between the Chukchi coast and the Kotzebue Sound and inland units of the study area, corresponding best to the nineteenth-century Inupiaq territories delineated by Ray (1984).

A singular discontinuity in the late-prehistoric settlement pattern associated with monumental architecture is interpreted to reflect conflict in a resource-rich boundary zone, possibly dating to the late 1700s and related to control of resources in a time of accelerated trade and climatic deterioration.

The picture that emerges on the northern Seward Peninsula during late prehistory corresponds well with broad regional trends identified in the Gulf of Alaska and the Northwest Coast. By the 1700s, people were on the move, boundaries were destabilized, and desire for control of scarce European trade items intensified both peaceful and hostile relations.

~~ Jeanne Schaaf

This summary is excerpted from an independent study (Schaaf 1995), which was not funded by the Shared Beringian Heritage Program, but was a companion to, and thus supported by, other late prehistoric archaeological research funded by the program.

REFERENCES CITED

Anderson, D.D.
1984   Prehistory of North Alaska. In *Handbook of North American Indians,* Vol.5, *Arctic,* D. Damas (ed.), pp. 80-93, Smithsonian Institution, Washington, D.C.

Arutiunov, S.A. and W.W. Fitzhugh
1988   Prehistory of Siberia and the Bering Sea, In *Crossroads of Continents: Cultures of Siberia and Alaska,* W. Fitzhugh and A. Crowell (eds.). Smithsonian Institution Press, Washington, D.C., pp.117-129.

Burch, E.S., Jr.
1974   Eskimo Warfare in Northwest Alaska. *Anthropological Papers of the University of Alaska* 16(2):1-14. Fairbanks.

1980   Traditional Eskimo Societies in Northwest Alaska. In *Alaska Native Culture and History,* Y. Kotani and W.B. Workman (eds.). National Museum of Ethnology, Senri Ethnological Studies 4, pp. 253-304, Osaka, Japan.

1984   Kotzebue Sound Eskimo. In *Handbook of North American Indians.* Vol. 5, *Arctic,* D. Damas (ed.), Smithsonian Institution, Washington, D.C., pp. 303-319.

1988   Toward a Sociology of the Prehistoric Inupiat: Problems and Prospects. In *Late Prehistoric Development of Alaska's Native People,* R. Shaw, R. Harritt, and D. Dumond (eds.). Aurora, Alaska Anthropological Association Monograph Series #4, pp. 1-16.

1988a   War and Trade. In *Crossroads of Continents: Cultures of Siberia and Alaska,* W. W. Fitzhugh and A. Crowell (eds.). Smithsonian Institution Press, Washington, pp. 227-240.

1994   The Cultural and Natural Heritage of Northwest Alaska, Volume V: The Inupiaq Nations of Northwest Alaska, Nana Museum of the Arctic, Kotzebue, Alaska, and National Park Service, Anchorage, Alaska.

Burch, E.S., Jr. and T.C. Correll
1972   Alliance and conflict: inter-regional relations in north Alaska. In *Alliance in Eskimo Society: Proceedings of the American Ethnological Society, 1971, supplement,* D.L. Guemple (ed.), University of Washington Press, Seattle, pp. 17-39.

Calkin, P. and G. Wiles
1990   Little Ice Age Glaciation in Alaska: A Record of Recent Global Climatic Change. In *Proceedings of International Conference on the Role of the Polar Regions in Global Change,* University of Alaska Fairbanks, 2:617-625.

Ferguson, B.R.
1983   Warfare and Redistributive Exchange on the Northwest Coast. In *The Development of Political Organizations in Native North America,* E. Tooker (ed.), pp. 133-147, The American Ethnological Society, Washington, D.C.

Foote, D.C.
1965   *Exploration and Resource Utilization in Northwestern Arctic Alaska Before 1855.* Unpublished Ph.D. dissertation, McGill University, Montreal.

Giddings, J.L.
1952   The Arctic Woodland Culture of the Kobuk River. *Museum Monographs,* University of Pennsylvania Museum, Philadelphia.

Giddings, J.L. and D.D. Anderson
1986   *Beach Ridge Archeology of Cape Krusenstern.* National Park Service Publications in Archeology 20, U.S. Government Printing Office, Washington, D.C.

Grove, J.M.
1988 *The Little Ice Age*. Methuen, London.

Hickey, C.G.
1979 The Historic Beringian Trade Network: Its Nature and Origins. In. Thule Eskimo Culture: An Anthropological Retrospective. A.P. McCartney (ed.), *National Museum of Man Mercury Series* No. 88:411-434, Ottawa.

Hodder, I.
1979 Economic and social stress and material culture patterning. *American Antiquity* 44:446-454.

Knecht, R.
1995 The Late Prehistory of the Alutiiq People: Culture Change on the Kodiak Archipelago from 1200-1750 A.D. (2 vols.). Ph.D. thesis, Bryn Mawr College.

Kotzebue, O. von
1821 *A voyage of discovery into the South Sea and Beering's Straits, for the purpose of exploring a north-east passage, undertaken in the years 1815-18*. 3 volumes. London: Longman, Hurst, Reese, Orme and Brown. Reprinted by N. Israel, Amsterdam, New York, 1967.

MacDonald, G.F.
1984 The Epic of Nekt. In *The Tsimshian Images of the Past: Views for the Present*, M. Seguin (ed.), pp.65-81, University of British Columbia Press, Vancouver.

1989 *Kitwanga Fort Report*. Canadian Museum of Civilization.

Mason, O.K. and S.C. Gerlach
1995 Chukchi Hot Spots, Paleo-polynyas, and Caribou Crashes: Climatic and Ecological Dimensions of North Alaska Prehistory. *Arctic Anthropology* 32(1):101-130.

Moss. M. and J. Erlandson
1992 Forts, Refuge Rocks, and Defensive Sites: The Antiquity of Warfare along the North Pacific Coast of North America. *Arctic Anthropology* Vol. 29: 2:73-90.

Oquilluk, W.A.
1981 *People of Kauwerak: Legends of the Northern Eskimo*. Alaska Pacific University Press, Anchorage.

Powers, Wm.R., J.A. Adams, A. Godfrey, J. Ketz, D. Plaskett and G.R. Scott
1982 *The Chukchi-Imuruk Report: Archaeological Investigations in the Bering Land Bridge National Preserve, Seward Peninsula, Alaska, 1974 and 1975*. Cooperative Park Studies Unit, Occasional Paper No.31, University of Alaska, Fairbanks.

Ray, D.J.
1964 Nineteenth Century Settlement and Subsistence Patterns in Bering Strait. *Arctic Anthropology* 2(2):61-94.

1967 Land Tenure and Polity of the Bering Strait Eskimos. *Journal of the West*, 6(3):371-394.

1975 *The Eskimos of Bering Strait, 1650-1898*. University of Washington Press, Seattle.

1984 Bering Strait Eskimo. In *Handbook of North American Indians*. Vol. 5, Arctic, D. Damas (ed.), Smithsonian Institution, Washington, D.C., pp. 285-302.

Schaaf, J.M.
1995 Late-Prehistoric Inupiaq Societies, Northern Seward Peninsula, Alaska: An Archeological Analysis AD 1500-1800, Ph.D. dissertation, University of Minnesota, Minneapolis.

***

(Opposite page)
Important aspects of culture such as language, clothing, and personal adornment that differentiate between groups are infrequently preserved in the archaeological record. ~ Painting by James Kivetoruk Moses, photographed by Trevor Roehl, courtesy of the Alaska State Museum (VA-538).

Stephen Igalukviaq, great-grandfather of Alex Weyiouanna and Walter Nayokpuk, is shown wearing his hairskin parka with a wolverine tail attached to the back. The attachment of tails and other animal parts to parkas symbolized Inupiaq beliefs. The garments influenced Siberian Natives to tell explorers that people to the east had tails.
~ Photo by Edward Keithahn, circa 1923, courtesy of Richard Keithahn (NPS neg. 029).

Excavations at Killak uncovered an intact tunnel entry to a house that had already eroded into the sea, August 1993. NPS archaeologist Steve Klingler (left) and Edgar Ningeulook.
~ Photo by Jeanne Schaaf.

(Opposite page)
Aerial view of rescue excavations at the early nineteenth century village site, Killak, which, according to Harvey Pootoogooluk, means place that goes around as in a bend, August 1993. Killak is extremely important because sites representing the period are largely absent from the record as a result of severe and rapid coastal erosion. State Office of History and Archaeology archaeologist Michele Jesperson (right) and Jeanne Schaaf. ~ Photo by James Magdanz.

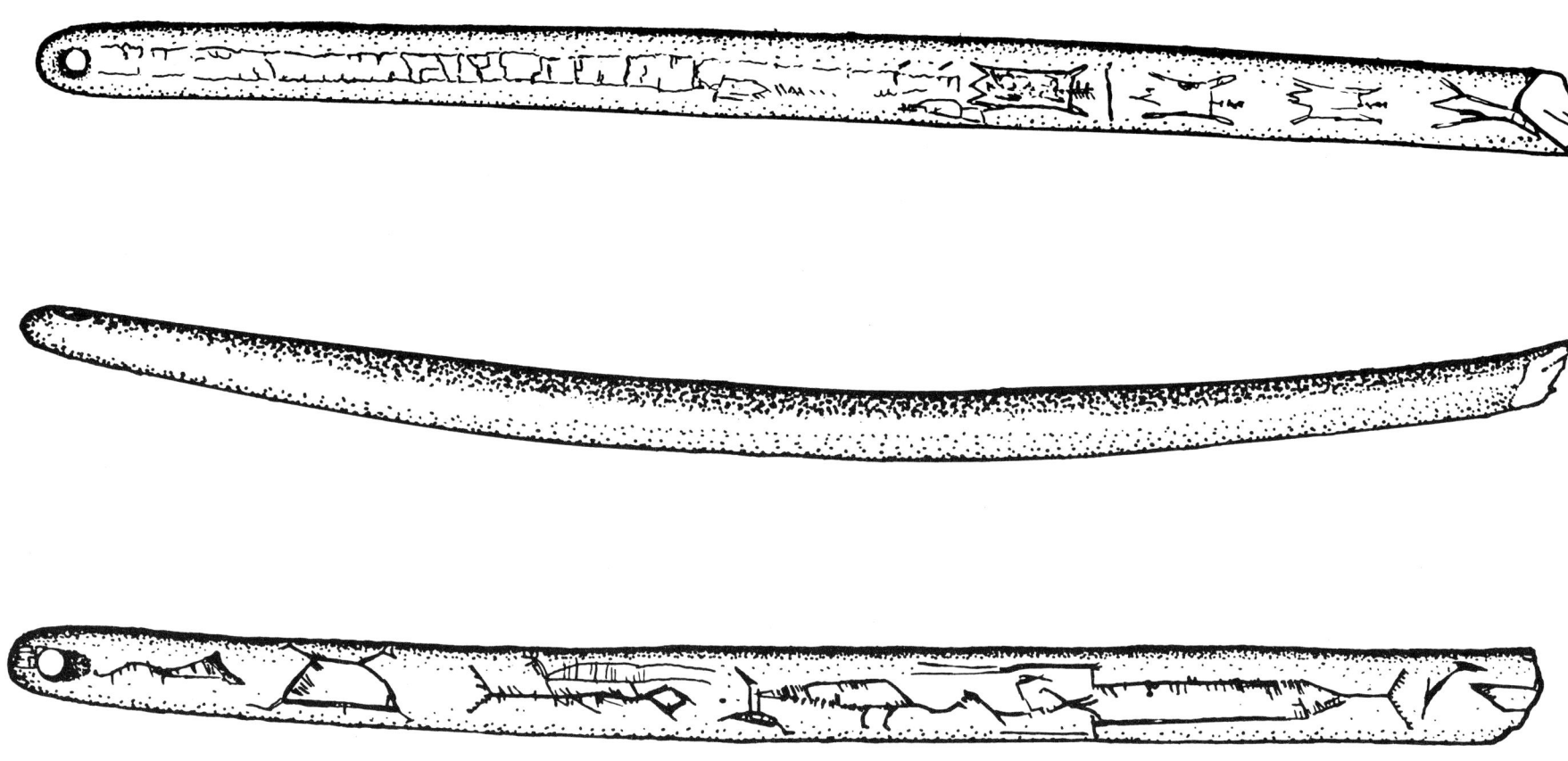

Piece of ivory bow drill found eroding from Killak village by NPS subsistence specialist Fred Tocktoo, August 1993. The reverse side (top) of the bow drill handle is incised with a series of symbols resembling fox pelts, indicating a people actively involved in the fur trade.
~ Drawing is actual size, by Frank Broderick.

In late summer of 1778, Captain James Cook and Lieutenant James King explored and named Norton Sound. Cook's reports document that the Inupiat had glass beads and "no dislike of tobacco" by 1778, ten years before the Anyui-Kolyma trade market was established.
~ Jeanne Schaaf.

"Three Friends" by James Kivetoruk Moses.
~ Photo by Trevor Roehl, courtesy of the Alaska State Museum (VA-553).

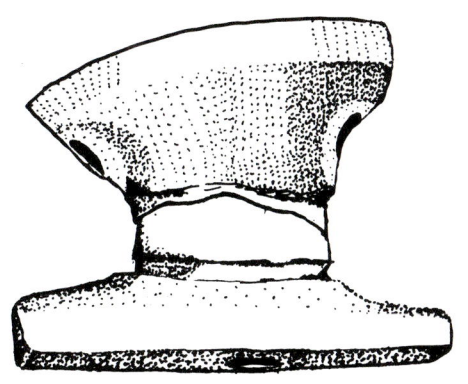

(Left) Drawing of carved white stone pipe bowl found at Killak, August 1993, actual size. Note similar pipe in use in above picture. ~ Drawing by Frank Broderick.

Kotzebue Sound Inupiat, sketched by Louis Choris, 1816.
~~ Photo by Chris Arend, courtesy of the Anchorage Museum of History and Art.

First European contact with the Seward Peninsula Inupiat north of Wales came with the voyage of Otto von Kotzebue in 1816 (Kotzebue 1821). On shore somewhere between Killak and Espenberg, they traded knives, looking-glasses, and tobacco for ivory carvings with a group of 50 men who arrived from the east (Espenberg) in five umiaks, later joined by several umiaks from the west (possibly Killak, Sinik, and/or Qivalauq). ~~ Jeanne Schaaf.

There was so much laughing and joking during the trading, that it appeared as if we were surrounded by the lively South Sea islanders, instead of the serious inhabitants of the north. Their arms consist of lances, bows, arrows, and a knife, two feet long, in a sheath; this military equipment, which they never lay aside, proves that they are in constant wars with other nations. Their lances, which are of iron, very well wrought, resemble those which the Russians have sold to the Tschukutskoi; the glass beads, also, with which they adorn themselves, are of the same kind as those worn in Asia, which proves that they must be in commercial intercourse with that continent.
(Kotzebue 1821:I:211)

Warfare is depicted on this ivory pipe stem. A battle rages outside while dancers celebrate unaware in the village ceremonial house. Enemy warriors have already stormed the entry shed; one villager is attempting to escape up a ladder into a high cache.
~ Photo by Chris Arend, courtesy of Anchorage Museum of History and Art (82.48.7).

Through millennia, intense frost action during glacial periods reduced the ancient lava flows to rubble, providing the building materials used by the Inupiat and their predecessors for shelter, hunting, meat storage, and large monuments, such as this unusual cairn on the summit of Twin Calderas. Cairn is 2.4 meters (8 feet) high.
~~ Photo by Jeanne Schaaf.

Stone monuments up to 3.5 meters tall (11.5 feet) on the rim of Twin Calderas, an ancient volcanic caldera in the Bering Land Bridge National Preserve.
~~ Photo by Jeanne Schaaf.

Unique flat-topped cairn at Twin Calderas. ~~ Photo by Jeanne Schaaf.

Atop Skeleton Butte, with commanding views in all directions, is a large village site with 25 rock-lined house depressions and 37 cache pits. Dave Hopkins is standing in one of three oval depressions along the east edge of the butte summit that may have been battle entrenchments, August 1995. ~~ Photo by Jeanne Schaaf.

The Hope and Promise of Ublasaun

(Opposite page)
Espenberg, at the mouth of the Espenberg River (Inuigniq, meaning no more people), is a settlement used seasonally for reindeer herding, hunting, and berry gathering, August 1993.
~~ Photo by James Magdanz.

It was the spring of 1918, and the world was embroiled in the closing phases of World War I. That was the year the tide of the war ultimately would turn to favor the allied forces. In contrast to that positive climate, however, during the coming winter 20 million people around the world would fall victim to a devastating epidemic of what was termed "Spanish influenza." While the war, removed by geography and culture from the day-to-day concerns of most Inupiat of Northwest Alaska, may have had little direct influence on their lives, the influenza epidemic to come would leave no one unaffected. The tumultuous political climate of the year passed unnoticed by Thomas Makaiqtaq Barr's first son, one-year old Gideon Kahlook Kunautaq Barr. Thomas' wife Emily Paizuzraq Kiyutelluk Barr had given birth to Gideon in the village of Shishmaref on July 21, 1917. Shishmaref was the location of women healers and midwives to whom Inupiat turned for assistance when giving birth. One of Gideon's Inupiaq names, Kahlook was bestowed upon him as a namesake of a deceased relative of his father. His other Inupiaq name, Kunautaq, was that of his father's father.

~~ Linda J. Ellanna and George Sherrod

From the perspective of Gideon Barr, his ancestors had lived in the Cape Espenberg area "from generation to generation, always..." (Barr 1988). After multiple deaths occurred at Nuiqtat, their winter village on Cape Espenberg, the entire Barr family moved about a mile distant, an indication of the traditional perspective of Makaiqtaq. Then, after the introduction of reindeer, the family moved further down the coast to establish the community Ublasaun, where they remained through 1925 or slightly longer. The move to Ublasaun guaranteed good pasturage for the deer and was also renowned as a site for seal netting. During the childhoods of Bessie Barr Cross and her brother Gideon Barr, travel during the winter was accomplished mainly by dog team and occasionally with sled deer. In the summer, people moved their family along the coast or upriver in skinboats with the herd. Makaiqtaq persisted in walking the land extensively for most of his life.

The settlement at Ublasaun extended about 2,000 feet from east to west along the sandy bluff, spanning the two small outlets of a tundra thaw lake. The houses, seven in all, were built from 1920 to 1922. There were also subsidiary structures, including pole caches, underground caches, boat racks, and dog stake-out yards. None of the structures was built more than 65 feet inland, a fact that threatens the entire abandoned community today with erosion.

Ties of both blood (consanguineal) and marriage (affinal) in this small community were of great importance. It was the local family that formed the bedrock of Ublasaun during traditional and transitional times. Local families were large bilaterally extended families encompassing several generations; they might include several married couples and their children, involve aged parents and sometimes grandparents (some of whom migrated into the community late in life), and provide the residence of numerous married siblings and cousins, sometimes removed to the second degree (Burch 1975:235-238). Ublasaun from 1920 to 1925 fit this description; and Makaiqtaq's extended local family predominated there. Ublasaun, because of its establishment specifically for reindeer herding, represented a blend of social factors -- not all of its inhabitants were members of the same society; and not all residents were closely related, although all eventually would be through marriage.

The west end of Ublasaun was dominated by the family of Makaiqtaq and Emily Paizuzraq Kiyutelluk Barr and their five children at that time: Fannie, Gideon, Elijah, Bessie, and Mary. Twins Martha and Susie, born between Fanny and Gideon, had died before the move to Ublasaun. Emily herself had close ties to the village of Kivalina, for she had spent time there with her parents Qinaqtuaq and Makluwiiq when she was a young girl and no doubt had relatives there. Makaiqtaq was born at Cape Espenberg and had spent at least a part of his youth at Sinik, near Ublasaun.

Makaiqtaq and Emily lived, as umialiq (strong man) and wife, in relative privacy at a prestigious location on the Ublasaun bluff, which would have been a good lookout for game and possibly the most prosperous seal-netting spot. The bluff also provided a source of recreation for the children. One of Gideon's fond memories is of sledding down the steep snowy sea cliffs and house mounds during the winter. He and his cousins would freeze a flensed sealskin and bend the front up into a prow, or find a suitable chunk of ice, then head wildly down the slope. The family also had the closest access to one of the two creeks that drained the nearby lake, guaranteeing easy launches for their boats and a good supply of fresh water.

There was at least one skinboat in Ublasaun at that time; and it belonged to Makaiqtaq, who would have employed his male kin as boat crew. There were six adult men in the community (Makaiqtaq, Sublaq, and Peter Kahlook [Qauqluk] Barr, Gordon Dimmick, James Kivetoruk Moses, and Lloyd Koonuk), two adult male elders whose ages are undetermined and who could have been retired from hunting (Qiluq and Umiaq), two boys who were probably teenagers (Adrian [also called Edwin] and Walter Barr), five boys between ages six and perhaps ten -- old enough perhaps to accompany the hunt but too young to be productive in it (Gideon, Roy, David, Rudolph, and Edward). This number of men and older boys would probably have been distributed most efficiently between two boats.

By then Makaiqtaq was the eldest living of the Barr siblings -- his eldest brother Ahvalook and his sister Quganaq having passed away. Another Barr brother, Peter Kahlook, lived just up the beach from Makaiqtaq with his family, Bessie Sikinguaq Okie Barr and their children Roy, David, and Lydia. Peter Barr had been adopted out to another family as a child, but had moved to Ublasaun sometime during this period to join his biological extended family in their reindeer enterprise. Adoption among the Inupiat, as has been discussed by Burch and others, is less an act of "giving up" a child than it is a sharing of family and an extension of kinship. So Peter Kahlook was still very much a part of the Barr extended family as well as that of his adopted kin, and both the act of his adoption and his return to his biologic family can be regarded as acts of sharing.

Just next door to Peter Kahlook and his family, Gordon Qiziilaaq Dimmick, an unmarried apprentice herder with kinship ties to Kivalina and Deering, lived in a small house. Dimmick, who had moved north from Qivaluaq (Kividlo) to help with the herd, probably shared his meals with Peter's family, as is the custom today with bachelors in Shishmaref. This proximity and familiarity, and perhaps the covert planning of a marital arrangement, probably contributed ultimately to the young apprentice's marriage to Bessie Sikinguaq Barr's sister Mary.

At the far northeastern end of the community, roughly half a mile from Makaiqtaq's home at a distance east of the second creek was the home of Gilbert (Sublaq) Barr, the second eldest of the Barr brothers, along his wife Rosie Umisaaq Barr and their four children: Lillian, Edward, Isaiah, and Jessie. If there were another skinboat in the community, it probably would have belonged to Gilbert or, perhaps, to Lloyd Koonuk. Between Sublaq's house and the second creek lived a number of relatives who had both consanguineal and affinal affiliations with Sublaq, his wife, and the rest of the community.

Very near the home of Sublaq and Rosie in a shared enclave of cache pits and elevated storage, was a tiny old-style home, which Gideon Barr describes as "...little, little, little, little!" that belonged to Rosie Barr's mother, Aguviuna, and stepfather, Umiaq. A daughter of Aguviuna's from a previous marriage also lived with the older couple along with an undetermined number of children. These residents had migrated down the coast to Ublasaun from an unknown location in the north, perhaps the Kivalina area where there are known to have been some kinship ties, presumably when times were lean or when they found that they no longer had close relations upon whom they could depend. By then word may also have traveled to other communities regarding the introduction and success of reindeer herding in the Cape Espenberg and Ublasaun area, although as newcomers would find, there were few literal profits to be made.

Umiaq and his wife were the only elders who lived full-time at Ublasaun. They served an important function in the teaching and socialization of the young people there, and their presence in that regard was welcome. Gideon Barr, in fact, had several mentors who served as grandfathers to him. One was Umiaq and another was Kanockdodt, Emily Kiyutelluk Barr's stepfather, the man that her mother Makluwiiq (Mary) had married after the accidental death of her husband, Kiyutelluk, just before Emily's birth. Makluwiiq's brother Charlie Teyeopuk Goodhope was also known as grandfather to Gideon Barr and his siblings. Goodhope had been one of the early reindeer apprentices and had moved north from Wales with his reindeer. Later, Makaiqtaq and Emily's eldest daughter Fannie was to marry Fred Goodhope, Charlie's son. Fannie's and Fred's daughter Shirley then married Clifford Weyiouanna, present-day herder and heir to the Allagiaq (Allockeok) reindeer dynasty through his mother Elsie Allockeok Weyiouanna. Fred Goodhope Jr. also married back into the cycle of Nuglunguktuk and Shishmaref Company herders, using Espenberg as his base today.

The Ublasaun elders discussed above helped young Gideon gain strength and prepare to be a hunter. At Espenberg, Gideon's maternal grandfather constructed toy bows for Gideon of ever-increasing size and strength, with which he play-hunted at Ublasaun and Cape Espenberg. Later, his grandfather began preparing a bow that would have been considerably more powerful than the toys. Lashed and strung with sinew around the front "so when you pull it, it'll give that much more tension [than] a plain wood one," the bow was to have been reminiscent of the sinew-backed bows that once had designated the most powerful communities and strongmen along the coasts, and was probably designed as a training exercise for young Gideon (Barr 1988). But his grandfather died before the bow was completed.

Because it would have been uncomfortable, if not impossible, for all members of a local family to fit into a single house, smaller "domestic family" groups lived in separate dwellings that were side by side and sometimes physically connected. This was the case at Ublasaun, where each structure or "household" was occupied by a single (although not necessarily nuclear) family.

Significantly, unmarried men and those whose direct connections to the Ublasaun extended family were fragmented by the death of close relations or other factors, appear to have lived at the center where they were literally and symbolically surrounded by more powerful kin.

Adrian and Walter Barr, sons of the deceased eldest Barr brother Ahvalook, lived near the second creek, where they probably performed chores such as hauling water for their uncle Sublaq, whose skinboat they may have crewed, and where they could eat and share in other ways with their relatives. These young men and several other families were "enclosed" by the security provided by their uncles at either end of the village and by their relationships with all. Other single men, such as herder Gordon Dimmick, were brought into the community and housed close to families into which they would later marry.

Between the homes of Makaiqtaq and the elders Umiaq and Aguviuna at Ublasaun, there were three other dwellings. The first house, moving east to west, was occupied by Adrian and Walter Barr. Moses Qiluq, whose deceased wife was Makaiqtaq's eldest sister Quganaq, lived in another small sod house with his adopted son James Kivetoruk Moses. Both were shareholders in the Nuglunguktuk herd.

Across the creek, next door to Peter Kahlook Barr, lived another family that included Lloyd Koonuk, his wife Margaret, and their children, Rudolph, Ernest, and Daisy. Margaret was the blood sister of James Kivetoruk Moses; their biological father had been the brother of widower Moses Qiluq. Koonuk himself, who was originally from the Arctic River area southwest of Shishmaref, was the brother of William Allockeok (Allagiaq) (Ellanna and Sherrod 1994). The ties of blood and marriage within the community were thus not only very complex, but extended out and drew in to and from other wealthy individuals, powerful local families, reindeer herds, regions, and Inupiaq nations through both male and female lineages.

The modest, efficient semi-subterranean dwellings described by Gideon Barr were constructed carefully and ingeniously, although, as Barr has pointed out, they could be completed very quickly, in as few as three or four days when necessary. If construction materials had been gathered previously, driftwood logs had already been split, and if "everybody pitched in together... everybody is willing to help each other, just like one family," the work went very quickly (Barr 1991). Housing for older people too infirm to build their own dwellings was constructed by others, usually very near their closest extended family members and therefore accessible to the same supplies and caches. In this sense, each local family (represented by Makaiqtaq and Emily Barr) functioned as a task group unit within extended family (Makaiqtaq, Sublaq, Kahlook Barr and others), community (Ublasaun) and finally, societal (Tapqaqmiut) and national (Inupiaq) entities.

Because the driftwood logs needed to build homes were heavy and bulky, requiring several adults to muscle them up the bluff to the building sites, houses were built communally whenever possible. And although an abundance of driftwood was obviously a key factor in house construction, builders also adapted to whatever was available. Some commercial materials, for example, may have been hauled in by barge or dog sled, but most were a product of recycling. Milled timbers, window sashes, doors, metal hinges, and nails were gleaned on a regular basis from the many shipwrecks in the area.

First, the main room of the house was cut about 4

feet into the ground out of a dune slope. By the time Ublasaun was established, commercial tools were being used, but previously, houses had been constructed with traditional implements including stone axes with wooden handles and a walrus scapula shovel. A driftwood spruce pole frame -- each pole notched with a U-shape to carry a 6-inch beam -- was then set up, creating a rectangular room with two gabled ends. The house framework at Ublasaun was built with split logs and a central driftwood ridgepole. Light thin round logs were used for the ceiling because they would rot before any other part and would permit easier repair or replacement.

The interior walls in the Barr house at Ublasaun were about 1.32 meters (4.36 feet) tall, composed of semi-circular, hewn-tapered, split driftwood slabs with the plank sides facing the interior, ninety-two pieces in all. More split driftwood slabs, one end notched to fit the hewn ends of the upright side wall slabs and the other resting on the log ridge beams were laid next to each other to form the roof of the dwelling. Each roof beam was apparently notched to receive the tapered end of the slabs. This method would have helped keep the roof slab from shifting, consequently resulting in a more solid structure. Blocks of sod were then layered over the roof and above-ground sides.

Hewn joints and notches were carefully crafted by the builders in the construction of the sod house. Support beams, floor planks, and other horizontal members were leveled using the expansive horizon of the sea as a reference. The builders of the sod house were able to construct a comfortable residence...by utilizing the natural compressive forces of the sand dune and sod covering to stabilize and protect the structure. Each log was beveled or pointed at both top and bottom; and although the hewn top clearly serves to anchor cross beams in the space between, there is no apparent reason for the beveling at the bottom. It is interesting to note that storm room ceilings, at roughly 1.59 meters (5.25 feet), were higher than the main room of the house, which would have served to trap some cold air.

The floor of the main room was a combination of planked driftwood and milled lumber, with commercial lumber predominating. Other milled lumber found in the site included a concentration of boards in the pantry, which was probably shelving, and a storage area of milled boards, as well as an abundance of artifacts under Makaiqtaq and Emily's bed (Sweeney 1994:4). House interiors were kept very spare, as many people often occupied a space that might have been only 150 feet square (13.50 meters square). There was no furniture, as such, although in the Barr home, two boxes used for storage and possibly seating, one manufactured from a Hill's Brothers coffee crate, were located on each side of the doorway.

Items like pots and pans, cooking utensils, and dishes were usually stored in the corner where the commercial stove was installed, although this may have been the purpose of the "pantry" ascribed to Makaiqtaq Barr's house. In the Barr home, chopped wood was stacked beside the stove. Kitchen areas were sometimes "domed," according to Barr, although he does not explain what he means -- certainly, the outer walls were lower than the gable peak. Tool boxes, carving tools, sewing boxes, and other tools and implements were stored out of the way, usually under a platform bed, whenever they were not in use, just as they are today. Women gathered in small related groups to sew and converse, while children -- especially girls -- crawled around the sewing materials and scraps, learning as they did so. The entryway itself offered other storage areas for both food and gear.

Makaiqtaq and Emily slept on a scrap lumber platform bed, while the children (with the exception of Bessie) slept on the floor. In earlier times, sleeping platforms had been covered with willows. The mattresses used when Gideon Barr was a boy were large canvas or heavy cloth bags sewn and stuffed with duck feathers or two reindeer hides, one with the hide down and one facing up. These were rolled up during the day and stored out of the way so other activities could take place. For the most part, privacy, as it is defined among Euro-Americans, was not only unavailable in these snug homes, it was undesired.

In the Barr home, Makaiqtaq and Emily Barr slept on a single-bed-size platform along an interior wall, while another space, 3 feet 2 inches by 6 feet 2 inches, which was attached at the southwest gable served as a sleeping loft for Bessie Barr. Her siblings, including Gideon, slept on the floor. Storage of personal items and things like sewing or carving materials was under the bunk. Another much smaller room is thought to have been a pantry, although Gideon does not remember for certain.

Because of their partly underground construction and sod exteriors, semi-subterranean homes were very warm, heated with seal oil lamps until the turn of the century in some areas and requiring only one or two lamps to heat a home of 150 square feet or more. Later, Coleman lamps took the place of traditional ones in many small homes.

Settlements like Ublasaun were kept as clean as possible, and refuse was never cached or dumped near residences. During the winter, trash of all types was set out on the sea ice so it would eventually drift away. But after the spring ugruk hunt, animal parts were burned at a site near the meat drying racks whenever a south wind blew. This practice, which carried the smoke and ash back out to the ocean, probably had ritual elements. As the ugruk and other animal fragments returned to the ocean, life-giving ties with sea mammals were acknowledged. This would have ensured future good hunting and reinforced important traditional beliefs that revolved around the continuing cycle of man-animal transformation.

As reindeer herding began to falter at Ublasaun, elders in the Barr extended family began to die, and residents of Ublasaun began to move on to other communities, the character of the extended family and the settlement itself changed. For a short time, Makaiqtaq and Emily lived in Deering, where their last child, Zaccheus William (Bill), was born. Then in 1937 when Makaiqtaq was nearly seventy, they moved back to the Tapqaq coast where he had spent time as a boy, choosing Sinik as their home, where they had spent the winters before establishing Ublasaun. Several sod houses were already established at Sinik, some of which had been built by other residents of Ublasaun. James Kivetoruk Moses established permanent residence at Sinik after his departure from Ublasaun and his marriage to Bessie. Gideon also built a home next to Moses' for his parents and built another for his own use in running traplines, although he never apparently intended to settle in the community. Other residents of Sinik included elders Joseph and Mary Eningowuk, who had been major reindeer owners in the Shishmaref Reindeer Company. The Eningowuks were important to Makaiqtaq and Emily, for they had a daughter of marriageable age. In time, they steered Gideon toward a marriage with Katherine Eningowuk, thus forming another alliance between families who had dominated the reindeer business throughout the region (Ellanna and Sherrod 1994:38).

Late in 1937, a fierce fall storm hit Sinik and other Tapqaq communities. It destroyed Makaiqtaq's skinboat, although no mention is made by Gideon Barr of the loss of any other boats. While the destruction caused a significant financial loss, it also signified the end of the self-reliant, entrepreneurial, and most influential period of Makaiqtaq's life. With the loss of the boat and the consequent inability to hunt ugruk efficiently, Makaiqtaq's ability to share hunted game would have been deeply damaged; and sharing was, and remains, the cornerstone of prestige and survival in Inupiaq society.

Makaiqtaq continued to garner the deep respect of his immediate and extended family and colleagues. When he and his family moved away from Ublasaun for good, they spent a brief period in Deering, where some of their children attended school sporadically and the older siblings and their father continued to run traplines and subsistence hunt.

With Makaiqtaq's death at about age 76 in 1945 at Shishmaref, the final chapter of his family's immediate involvement in reindeer herding and the early history of reindeer herding at Cape Espenberg and Ublasaun also came to a close. During that period Gideon Barr had hired on in Nome with Glen Carrington and Company, working as a clerk, stocker, and longshoreman on a three year contract. When his father fell ill, he hurried back to Shishmaref. Makaiqtaq's final request of his eldest son, whom he had trained to be primary hunter, trapper, and herder was this, as told by Gideon:

My father sent for me.
He requested I go home.
His health was not good.
His breathing was bothering him--
he was short of breath.
Because of respect, I went home.
It was certainly true.

Right after I reached home, he spoke:
"I am longing for reindeer fawn meat,"
he said.
We cast our skinboat into the water.
Pagik was my companion at that time.
He and I went to Niglanaqtuuq River.

He and I were stranded for one week there
because of northeasterly winds.

We butchered right away.
But while I was gone, my father died.
When he died they laid him to rest.
I went home, but he was gone!
Then, my mother said to me,
"We laid him to rest right away."
I grieved then.
When I was getting the food he wanted,
then he was missing.
With this story --
It is the first story.
I am telling you.
(Gideon Barr 1982)

~ Susan W. Fair, James Creech,
Gideon K. Barr Sr., and Edgar Ningeulook

REFERENCES

Barr, Gideon K. Sr.
1993 Tape-recorded interview (in Inupiaq) by Susan W. Fair and Edgar Ningeulook, Shishmaref, AK. 2 August 1993. Translated and transcribed by Fred Tocktoo, finalized by Edgar Ningeulook. U.S. Department of the Interior, National Park Service, Alaska System Support Office. Shared Beringian Heritage Program, Anchorage, Alaska.

1993a Videotaped interview. Taylor Productions, Inc. August 1993. On file at National Park Service, Anchorage, Alaska.

1991 Tape-recorded interview by James Simon and Jeanne Schaaf. Transcribed by Herbert O. Anungazuk, 21 September 1991. Audiotape, Shishmaref, Alaska. U.S. Department of the Interior, National Park Service, Alaska System Support Office. Shared Beringian Heritage Program, Anchorage, AK.

1991a Tape-recorded interview by Ernest S. Burch Jr. and Igor Krupnik. Transcribed by Michael Faugno, 11 July 1991. Audiotape, Shishmaref, AK. U.S. Department of the Interior, National Park Service, Alaska System Support Office. Shared Beringian Heritage Program, Anchorage, AK.

1991b Tape-recorded interview by Ernest S. Burch Jr. . Transcribed by Michael Faugno and Sarah McGowan, 12 July 1991, Shishmaref, AK. U.S. Department of the Interior, National Park Service, Alaska System Support Office. Shared Beringian Heritage Program, Anchorage, AK.

1991c Tape-recorded interview by Ernest S. Burch Jr. Transcribed by Michael Faugno, 16 July 1991. Audiotape, Shishmaref, AK. U.S. Department of the Interior, National Park Service, Alaska System Support Office. Shared Beringian Heritage Program, Anchorage, AK.

1991d Tape-recorded interview by Herbert O. Anungazuk (in Inupiaq). Translated by Herbert O. Anungazuk, rewritten by Michael Faugno, 18 July 1991. Audiotape, Shishmaref, AK. U.S. Department of the Interior, National Park Service, Alaska System Support Office. Shared Beringian Heritage Program, Anchorage, AK.

1988 "Gideon Barr's Place Names, Espenberg." Self tape-recorded interview. Transcribed by Mary Ann Roddy and edited by Herbert O. Anungazuk. Bureau of Indian Affairs (BIA). ANCSA tape 88-ESP-005 to 88-ESP-011, BIA. Anchorage, Alaska.

1987 Three tape-recorded interviews by Jeanne Schaaf. Transcribed by Mary Ann Roddy, edited by Herbert O. Anungazuk, 15-16 May 1987. Nome, Alaska. U.S. Department of the Interior, National Park Service, Alaska System Support Office.

1982 Eskimo Heritage Program No. SH-AN-82-004-Tape 1. Tape-recorded interview by Albert Ningeulook 2 February 1982; translated and transcribed by Albert Ningeulook. Retranslated by Edgar Ningeulook for NPS, 1994. Kawerak, Inc., Nome, AK, Eskimo Heritage Program.

1982a Eskimo Heritage Program No. SH-AN-82-005-T1-#5. Tape-recorded interview by Albert Ningeulook (n.d.) February 1982; translated and transcribed by Albert Ningeulook. Retranslated by Edgar Ningeulook for NPS, 1994. Kawerak, Inc., Nome, AK, Eskimo Heritage Program.

1937 Letter from Barr, Shishmaref, Alaska, to J. Sidney Rood, Acting General Reindeer Superintendent, Nome, Alaska. 28 December 1937. National Archives, Alaska Region. Record Group No. 75, Bureau of Indian Affairs, Box 47, Alaska Reindeer Service, File: 156.8, Nuglunguktuk.

N.D. *William Allokeok*. Unpublished essay on file at ABE Learning Center, Shishmaref, Alaska.

Barr, Fanny Kigrook and Gideon K. Barr Sr.
1993 Tape-recorded interview by Susan W. Fair and Edgar Ningeulook. Transcribed and translated (original in Inupiaq) by Fred Tocktoo and Edgar Ningeulook, 4 August 1993, Shishmaref, Alaska. U. S. Department of the Interior, National Park Service, Alaska System Support Office. Shared Beringian Heritage Program, Anchorage, AK.

Barr, Makaiqtaq (Thomas), et al.
1929   *History of the Cape Espenberg Herd of Reindeer,* July 18, 1929, Nunagayok River. Anchorage, AK: National Archives, Alaska Region, Records of the Alaska Reindeer Service, Record Group No. 75, Box No. 47, Location 05/05/12(1), General Case Files, Northwestern Unit Manager, Pilot Station, File: Nuglunguktuk.

Burch, Ernest S. Jr.
1975   Eskimo Kinsmen: Changing Family Relationships in Northwest Alaska. Monographs of the American Ethnological Society 59. St. Paul, MN: West Publishing Company.

Creech, James E.
1995   Description of Historic Structures at Ublasaun, Bering Land Bridge National Preserve. Unpublished report on file at National Park Service, Anchorage, Alaska.

Cross, Bessie (Elizabeth)
1993   Tape-recorded interview by Susan W. Fair; transcribed by Edgar Ningeulook, 30 July 1993. Kotzebue, Alaska. U.S. Department of the Interior, National Park Service, Alaska System Support Office. Shared Beringian Heritage Program, Anchorage, AK.

1988   Tape-recorded interview by Brian Hoffman and David Staley; tran scribed by Mary Ann Roddy, 26 May 1988. Kotzebue, Alaska. Bureau of Indian Affairs (BIA) ANCSA tape 88-ESP-003, BIA, Anchorage, Alaska.

Ellanna, Linda J. and G. Sherrod
1994   "From Hunters to Herders: The Transformation of Earth, Society, and Heaven Among the Inupiat of Beringia." Draft manuscript on file at the National Park Service, Anchorage, Alaska.

Fair, Susan W. and E. N. Ningeulook
1995   "Qamani: Up the Coast, in My Mind, in My Heart." Manuscript on file at National Park Service, Anchorage, Alaska.

Keithahn, Edward
1923   *Eskimo Adventure: Another Journey into the Primitive.* Seattle: Superior Publishing Co.

Sweeney, Mary A.
1994   Excavations and Analysis of a 1920s Historic Inupiat Reindeer Herder's Winter House. Master's thesis. Department of Anthropology, University of Alaska Fairbanks.

From left, Bessie Barr Cross; her mother, Emily Paizuzraq Kiyutelluk Barr; and Bessie's older sister, Fannie Barr Goodhope, in Kotzebue, 1970.
~~ Photo by Mary Sue (Cross) Anderson.

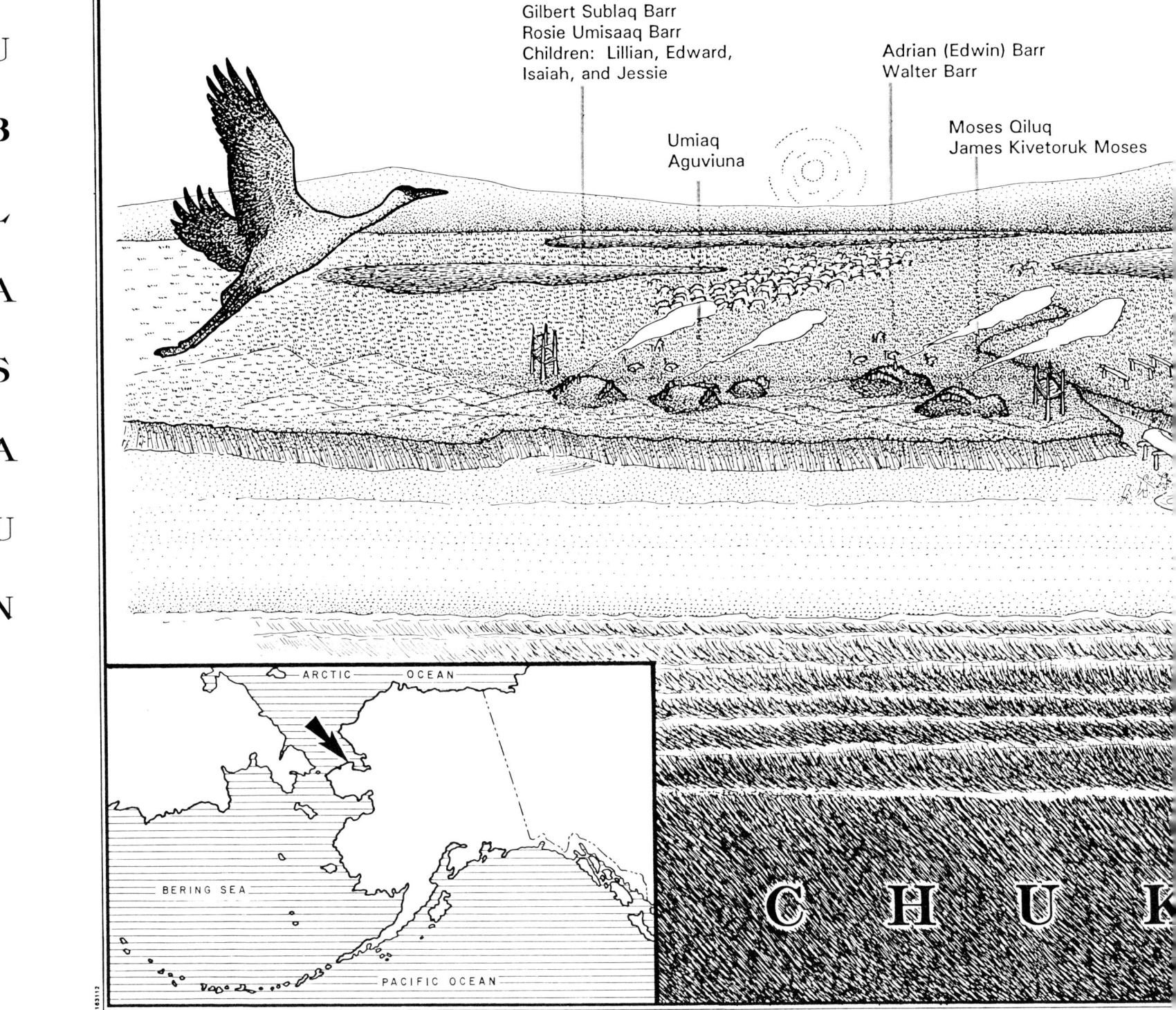

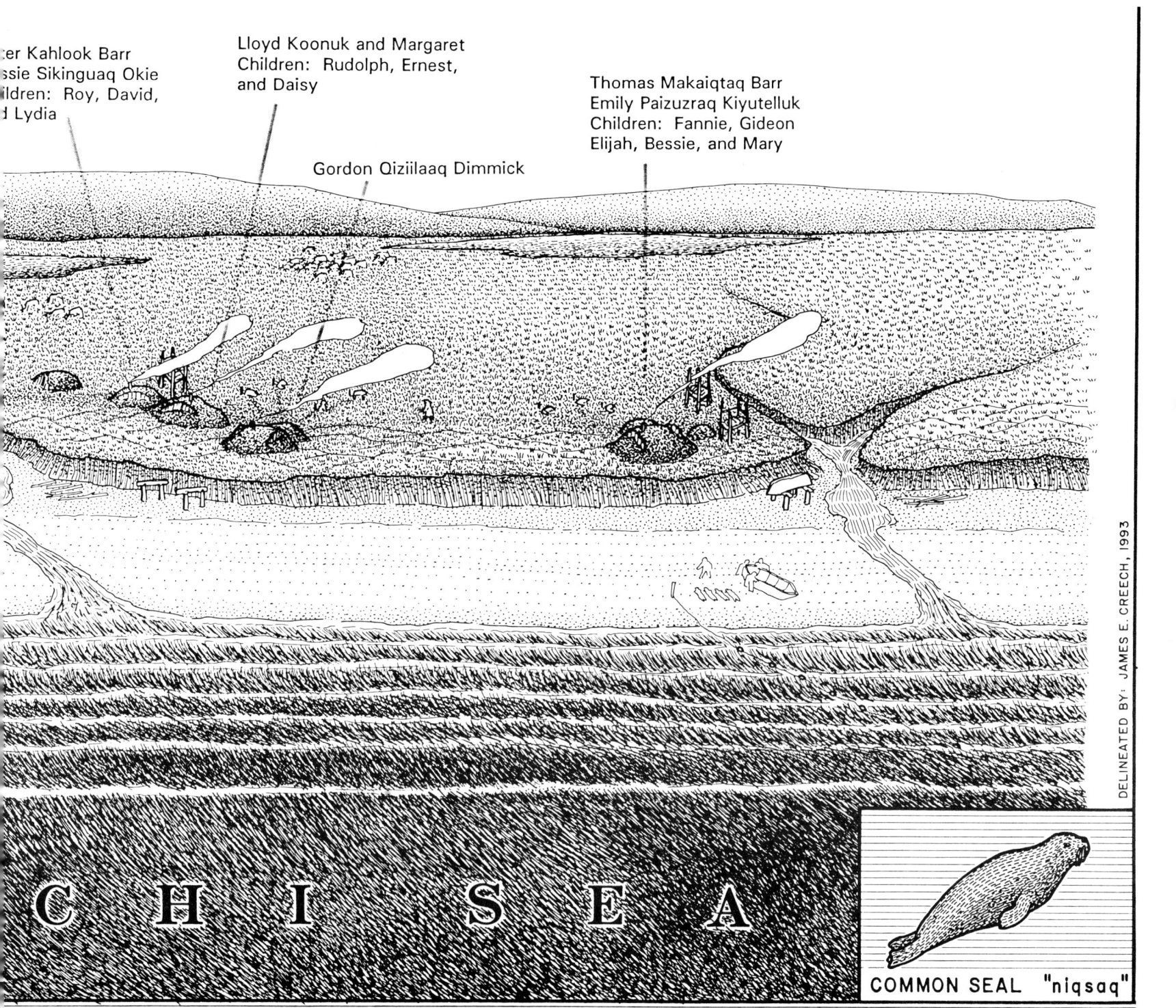

Gilbert Sublaq Barr's wife, Rosie Umisaaq, is shown here with their children Lillian, Edward, Isaiah, and Jessie, probably on a visit to Shishmaref from their home at Ublasaun.
~~ Photo by Edward Keithahn, circa 1923, courtesy of Richard Keithahn and National Park Service (neg. 061).

Emily Paizuzraq Kiyutelluk Barr, wife of Makaiqtaq Barr and mother of Gideon Barr and Bessie Barr Cross, 1960. The strips of wolverine fur, called "tails," on her parka signified wealth.
~~ Photo taken in Kotzebue by Dave Walluk, courtesy of Mary Sue (Cross) Anderson.

When I was a girl, my grandmother (Emily Barr) lived next door to us in Kotzebue, and my brother and I would take turns sleeping with her. I remember waking up to the sound of her singing. She was always singing, especially church songs in Inupiaq. I would snuggle under her down comforter in the morning while she sang as she made coffee and hot cakes to take next door for our breakfast. I was very fond of her. ~~ Mary Sue (Cross) Anderson.

Mary Quzraun (Cross) Ahgupuk, known as Mizugnaat, poses for the camera in a traditional fancy squirrelskin parka with the U-shaped hem common to feminine garments. Mizugnaat, an outstanding skinsewer, lived alone in a small sod house after her husband's death, practicing as a traditional healer known as a "feeler" and midwife. She was a powerful woman who served on the Traditional Council in Shishmaref at the critical time of the influenza epidemic.
~~ Photo by Edward Keithahn, circa 1923, courtesy of Richard Keithahn and National Park Service (neg. 056).

Emily Paizuzraq Barr often attended the spring whaling festival, Nalukataq, at Point Hope. Emily was raised at Cape Espenberg, but her family had close ties to Point Hope and Kivalina. ~ Photo by Frank H. Whaley, circa 1955, courtesy of Arctic Circle Enterprises, Inc. and Mary Sue (Cross) Anderson.

James Kivetoruk Moses, shown with an unidentified child, displays an arctic fox skin for the photographer, Edward Keithahn. Keithahn noted that local Inupiaq trappers earned far more than the schoolteachers.
~~ Photo by Edward Keithahn, circa 1923, courtesy of Richard Keithahn and National Park Service (neg. 078).

Bessie Ahgupuk, sister of the artist George Ahgupuk, married James Kivetoruk Moses. She was a schoolteacher in Shishmaref for many years and then accompanied her husband to Nome.
~~ Photo by Edward Keithahn, circa 1923, courtesy of Richard Keithahn and National Park Service (neg. 218).

Two unidentified boys wearing knee-high waterproof boots gather netted seals from the beach, probably in the fall since no ice is visible. The spotted seal appears to have been damaged on the neck and chest by the net. Children at Ublasaun once raced out each morning to claim seals that had drifted in from the nets and bring them to their families.
~~ Photo by Edward Keithahn, circa 1923, courtesy of Richard Keithahn and National Park Service (neg. 008).

A Short Story about Ublasaun and How It Was Used

This is a short story concerning this reindeer camp
    and how it was used.

In the fall, our fathers would connect their seal nets together
    in order to make a longer line net.
The short side of the net is attached with rawhide
    tied up to the mainland,
        and the outside ends always have heavy anchors.
That's how they set their sealing nets out before freeze-up
    around starting in September, middle part,
        until the ocean starts freezing in early October.
It's a real successful place for seal hunting with nets
    before freeze-up.

And whenever the ocean is calm,
    that's when they haul their seal net up.
And during the storm, while the ocean is rough,
    too rough to go out with a skin boat,
        some seals that were caught in the net and drowned...
If they have already drowned,
    those waves would work them loose from the net,
        and they would drift ashore on the beach.
That's when it's either northeast to north wind,
    or the west wind—
That's when this place gets awful rough
    to where the boats can't go out to haul in the nets.

Early in the morning,
    people would be busy trying to beat each other to find
    some seals drifted ashore either side of the camp there.
Because they always spread along the beach
    when they've drifted ashore.
The first one is always lucky—
Either way out on the east side or on the west side.
And that's how our fathers have always been hunting
    with seal nets before freeze-up.

Of course, those seal nets are all made out of rawhides out of
    seal skin.
That's for netting.
And for the upper cork line or lower lead lines,
    the rawhide are made out of ugruk skin cut into strips.
So these are made for real strong rope only
    and that's what they use—mostly.
You hardly ever see any manila rope
    or white man kind of rope them days...
You will see only the people that can afford to pay for them
    always have them.
And lots of Natives are using rawhides for work,
    even for dogteam tug lines and so forth.

And the younger people—
During winter they would have broken in new young wild
    deers and trained them into sled deers.
That's how these younger people do their work
    as the herder and trainers.
A real successful herder at least would train
    two to three sled deers a winter.
Of course, it takes time, every day,
    as long as the weather is good, they have to train them.
Try and use them like a dog with a sled.

And these people don't have too much experience
    or are handling them too rough.
[They] always barely make one that is useable as a sled deer.
The animals have to be treated right, not with rough work.
Those are the ones that are always more successful.
Of course, you've gotta have more power
    than the reindeer that you are training.
You've gotta be stronger in order to handle him
    around while training.
And it don't take too long for some people
    to train their sled deers.
Which, today, you don't even see, nowadays...
As many reindeer herders [as there are] in Seward Peninsula,
    none of them have sled deer in today's time.

That's how the people have been living in the past.
And, during the winter, they always use a little short net
    which they set for seals, seal nets,
        hardly six-feet long to set under the cracks—
These are old cracks that have been frozen over.
As long as there's some breathing holes
    on those cracks, that means there are some seals
        traveling, living in that crack.
And [hunting] will always be very successful after January.
Starting February and March are the best months
    to have those seal skin nets set under the ice.
Those seal nets, what I'm talking about,
    are still in use at today's time,
        but very few people only use them.

But I have some seal nets that I have kept.
What my father made before he died.
He tried to keep them as a souvenir.
Those are made out of seal skin rawhide and the rest
    are made out of cotton in the earlier days.
Now, in today's time, you got the material that is made
    out of nylon...
Ropes which don't rot in the water, which,
    they are real successful.
Nylon netting will outlast most any nets as long as
    you don't lose them out in the big storm.

Sometimes everybody loses their seal nets that are set on the same crack when
    that ice starts piling up, according to the big storms...
That's a time when people lost [everything] under the ice...
Not every year, but sometimes.
If you choose a place where the ice is not too thick,
    this will easily happen.
They are always look[ing] for a good place to set,
    looking for big thick heavy ice.
That's the ice that don't easily move around too much,
    don't break up too easy during the big storms.

~~ Gideon Kahlook Barr Sr., Shishmaref, Alaska, 1988

Bessie Sikinguaq Okie Barr and her children Roy, Lydia, and David, are shown at Shishmaref. Several portraits of women in Makaiqtaq Barr's extended family were taken by Edward Keithahn, suggesting that the women may have spent time in town while their husbands were at Ublasaun. Bessie Okie was originally from Cape Espenberg; she lived with her husband, Peter Kahlook at Ublasaun, where Kahlook joined in the reindeer herding venture with his older brother.
~~ Photo by Edward Keithahn, circa 1923, courtesy of Richard Keithahn and National Park Service (neg. 018).

These Shishmaref men are checking seal nets by umiaq in the fall. Shoreline ice at this time of year can be 12-15 feet high, formed by blowing spray. The weather and the task require waterproof garments; four of the men are wearing kavutaq, seal intestine parkas. Fred Tocktoo notes that the first man is getting up to secure the umiaq, "ready to haul in," the second has a tarp or spray guard on his lap, and the captain (at the rear) is wielding a large steering oar and wearing sealskin pants.
~ Photo by Edward Keithahn, circa 1923, courtesy of Richard Keithahn and National Park Service (neg. 004).

Flora Walluk Sagoonick (Sagna) poses with a prize reindeer in Shishmaref. She is wearing a fancy, carefully tailored, spotted-reindeer skin parka. The tusk-shaped white gores on the front of the garment are typical of northwest Alaska. In the background, from the left are teachers' quarters, school (between antlers), and traditional semi-subterranean houses.
~~ Photo by Edward Keithahn, circa 1923, courtesy of Richard Keithahn and National Park Service (neg. 115).

Holly Nayokpuk (Sockpick) and Delores (Barr) are shown playing with a skin ball. Such balls were usually stuffed with reindeer hair and were sometimes appliqued with dyed skin strips in geometric patterns or with tufts of unborn seal hair.
~ Photo by Edward Keithahn, circa 1923, courtesy of Richard Keithahn and National Park Service (neg. 108).

This reindeer corral used in the Shishmaref area has deer impaled on the driftwood fence.
~~ Photo by Edward Keithahn, circa 1923, courtesy of Richard Keithahn and National Park Service (neg. 113).

A reindeer is branded while children look on, probably at one of William Allockeok's reindeer corrals.
~ Photo by Edward Keithahn, circa 1923, courtesy of Richard Keithahn and National Park Service (neg. 124).

Five-mile reindeer corral, Shishmaref Company, circa 1923.
~~ Photo by Edward Keithahn, circa 1923, courtesy of Richard Keithahn and National Park Service (neg. 045).

Carson Tingook, father of Fannie Kuzuguk, shown here leading a sled deer, is remembered as an accomplished sled builder and a mentor in ivory carving to many local men.
~~ Photo by Edward Keithahn, circa 1923, courtesy of Richard Keithahn and National Park Service (neg. 120).

~ *With Thomas' death and the demise of the Nuglunguktuk Reindeer Company, the hope and promise of Ublasaun were gone. The following summer, baby boy Thomas Makaiqtaq Barr was born to Gideon and Katherine.* ~
~~ Linda J. Ellanna and George Sherrod

Gideon Barr and his first wife, Katherine Eningowuk Barr, are shown here holding reindeer bells in March 1938. Katherine's parents, elders Joseph and Mary Eningowuk of Sinik, were once major reindeer owners in the Shishmaref Reindeer Company. The Barr and Eningowuk marriage forged one of many alliances between families who dominated the reindeer business throughout the region.
~~ Photo courtesy of Gideon Barr, reproduced by James Magdanz.

NPS historic architect James Creech is shown here recording construction details in the ruins of Makaiqtaq Barr's home at Ublasaun, July 1991. ~ Photo by Jeanne Schaaf.

Makaiqtaq Barr's home at Ublasaun, as it may have looked when occupied in the early 1920s. ~ Drawing by James Creech.

Cutaway view of Thomas Makaiqtaq Barr's home at Ublasaun, showing details of construction. ~ Drawing by James Creech.

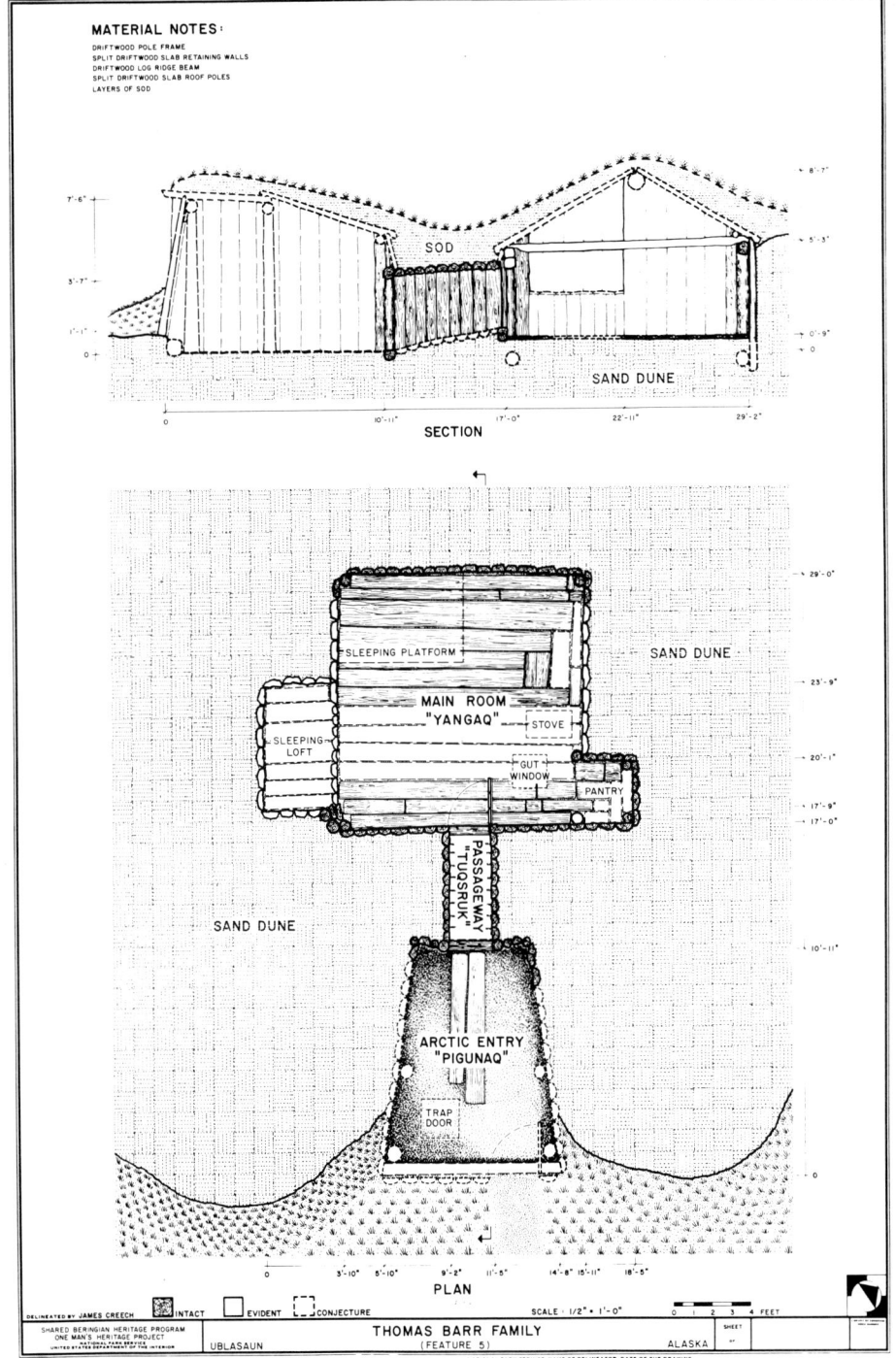

This rendering by James Creech of the profile and plan view of Thomas Makaiqtaq Barr's home at Ublasaun represents the first architectural documentation of historic Native architecture in Alaska, according to the standards of the NPS Historic American Buildings Survey.

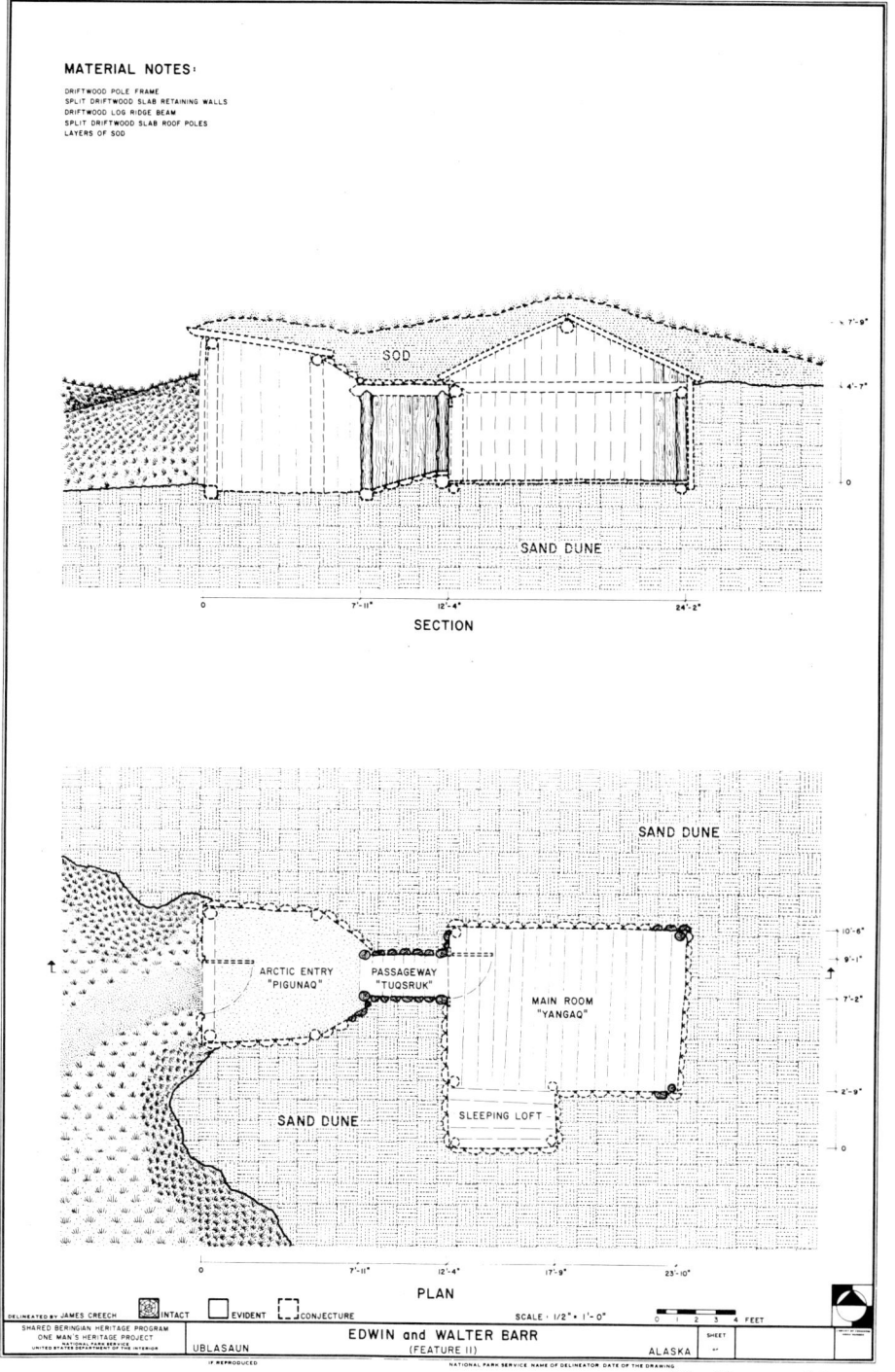

Profile and plan view of Adrian (Edwin) and Walter Barr's house at Ublasaun, drawn by James Creech.

This Kivetoruk Moses painting tells of the meeting of two powerful men, one a shaman and the other the captain of the cutter *Bear*. The captain and his mate go ashore, where the mate challenges the shaman to a rope-and-string trick. The shaman, suspicious of the men, decides to stage a dramatic event; and, calling upon the white men to imitate him, he stabs himself, whereupon the captain and his mate depart hastily for the ship, which was anchored at Port Clarence sealing camp.
~~ By James Kivetoruk Moses. ~~ Photo by Trevor Roehl, courtesy of the Alaska State Museum (VA-169).

Historical Archaeology and the Early Twentieth Century Reindeer Herding Frontier on the Northern Seward Peninsula, Alaska

By the last decade of the nineteenth century the Euro-American frontier had expanded to the far shores of the Bering Sea. On the heels of Russian, British, and American fur traders came the Yankee whalers, gold seekers, merchants, and profiteers who turned the failure and success of others into small and large fortunes. By the early twentieth century Alaska was a final frontier for a Euro-American ideology and global economy, a final stage for the expansion and imposition of a New World order that began on the eastern seaboard in the fifteenth century and slowly but surely moved westward across the continent. As the centuries changed, so changed the lives of the Inupiat of Northwest Alaska. The incorporation of reindeer and the Euro-American imposition of a pastoral way of life on Native Alaskans was an integral part of the colonization process.

A continuing American commitment to the ideology of the frontier notwithstanding, western scholars have long debated the substance and applicability of the concept since it was popularized by Frederick Jackson Turner in 1893. Turner did not invent the frontier; but he did formalize and legitimize a symbol used by politicians and profiteers to stabilize an economic system, justify the removal of indigenous Americans from traditional lands, and to unite a nation recovering from the Civil War. Indigenous people throughout the world experienced frontier and global colonization in ways that are remarkably similar; the North American case is little different in this regard. Although many indigenous North Americans were removed from ancestral lands and resettled on foreign ground, or were at least restricted and limited in their movements to comparatively small reservations in their home country, the colonization of Alaska was played out entirely within terrain long occupied by indigenous groups. Rather than conquests through military campaigns, Americans employed a conscious policy of assimilation of Native Alaskans primarily through education.

The Native northwest Alaskan was no stranger to the presence of foreign people, goods, and gods, experiencing first the Russian and the British fur trade, then the sustained impact of the American fur trade, the gold rush, and finally the sustained efforts of Euro-American expansion and colonization. Nor were they strangers to trade, with well established and sustained trading contacts and networks linking Northwest Alaska with the people of Siberia on the west, Yupik to the south, and the Athapaskans of Alaska and Canada. They were, however, strangers to the idea of herding rather than hunting reindeer.

Two perspectives on the nature of the frontier help us understand the impact of the introduction of reindeer on the indigenous people of Northwest Alaska. A frontier, in a geographical sense, is a "zone of contact between two contrasting types of land use, where the bearers of a new and different way of using natural resources advance, displacing older, indigenous, modes and peoples" (Jordan 1993:7). A frontier, in a cultural sense, is a zone of conflict between two or more contrasting cultures, each with a different ideology, perception of landscape, and strategy of land use. While frontiers commonly expand, contract, and remain stable for variable periods of time, they still commonly place individuals and groups in relation to vast economic, trade, exploitative, industrial, military, and transportation network. Colonization in any form alters old and creates new cultural and ecological landscapes upon which humans must operate, involving as it does the interaction of multiple societies, both intrusive and indigenous.

Much, of course, has been written about the history, the strategy, the motivation, and justification for the introduction of reindeer from the Euro-American point of view. Relatively little has been written about the way in which Inupiat and families adjusted to, incorporated, accepted and rejected the goods, services, material "wealth," and the problems and prospects of foreign hegemony, or dominance, over familiar places and people from an archaeological or material point of view. There is little in the literature that connects the individual to the wider society through analysis of the way that traditional places and settlements were used and abandoned, the manner in which participation in a wider social and ecological arena is reflected in the material record, of the way in which indigenous individuals and groups participated in the economic opportunities and constraints of the Euro-American expansion, or of the way that everyday life was experienced from the "bottom up" rather than from the "top down."

Life at the "outer edge of the wave—the meeting point between savagery and civilization" (Turner 1921), while an unfortunate image from the vantage of the late twentieth century, still reflects the attitude with which Sheldon Jackson, Presbyterian minister and chief proponent of an Alaskan Native reindeer industry, established his niche as an agent of change for church and state. The subtle imposition of a political and economic order, education, ideology, and religion as part of the colonial enterprise, rather than conquest through a series of wars, contrasts the Alaska frontier with the history of westward, colonial expansion through the rest of North America (Worster 1994). Regardless of how the relationship is perceived, the Inupiat of northwestern Alaska were participants in the local, national, and international arena, a landscape that involved both European and American forces and influences.

By the last decades of the nineteenth century, the Inupiat of Northwest Alaska experienced famine, disease, and social change, and a precipitous decline in their most important subsistence resources (Fortuine 1992). Yankee whalers seriously depleted walrus and whale stocks, and by 1900 caribou had declined or been absent from the country for years (Bockstoce 1986). In September 1890, the Presbyterian minister Sheldon Jackson urged the commissioner of the U.S. Bureau of Education to import reindeer into Alaska in an effort to benefit what he perceived to be a destitute Native population of the Territory (Stern et al. 1980). After his brief arctic tour, Jackson concluded that the introduction of reindeer would save the "Eskimos" from starvation, serve the purpose of providing industrial education, and promote cultural and spiritual well-being (Stern et al. 1980: 24). Jackson was certainly not the first to promote reindeer in this manner, but he was one of the most vocal and most influential spokesman for this cause. Although he was unable to convince Congress to underwrite the project, he was able to secure sufficient funds from the public to import 16 reindeer from Siberia in 1891, another 171 in 1892, and more than 1,000 over the following 10 years.

Late nineteenth and twentieth century accounts and histories of the reindeer industry can be read in many ways, although most reflect Euro-American voices and perspectives. Superficially, the history of reindeer herding can be divided into three developmental phases. For the first 22 years of the industry's existence, reindeer ownership was controlled primarily by the government and the missions, a few Saami, and a few wealthy Inupiat. After 1914, the pattern of ownership changed as American entrepreneurs such as the Lomen family entered and began to dominate the industry. This period of commercial exploitation lasted until 1939. The reindeer proliferated to the point where overgrazing had become a serious problem, new herds had been established in marginal areas, and the pattern of Native ownership had shifted from individual to joint-stock ownership systems and reindeer associations. Throughout this period the commercial aspects of the reindeer industry were secondary to the governmental intention of establishing a self-sustaining Native enterprise (Stern et al. 1980: 16).

The Cape Espenberg Inupiat were clearly active reindeer herders; but they incorporated reindeer in their own way, according to their own customs, and with their own response to governmental rules and regulations. The Espenberg Inupiat at times behaved like hunter-gatherers with domesticated reindeer, at times like pastoralists who hunted and gathered, and at times like reindeer ranchers who also had a penchant for the pursuit, capture, and consumption of sea mammals and fish.

Gideon Barr, an Inupiaq elder, contributed heavily to a recent historical archaeology study of the area as our study was in many ways a window into his life and the life of his family from about 1918 to 1925. The study, now nearing completion, presents the results of investigations at four specific locations used by the Barr family, a reindeer herding winter village, a spring camp, a summer camp, and a reindeer corral and camp complex. Those sites represent places used during a seasonal round by the same group of reindeer herders over a span of about 20 years or so.

During a brief period of fieldwork in the summer of 1991, Jim Simon and I, accompanied by Jeanne Schaaf, an archaeologist from the National Park Service, and an ethnographic team composed of Linda Ellanna, George Sherrod, Ernest S. Burch Jr., and Igor Krupnik, visited and conducted preliminary interviews with Gideon Barr and others in

Shishmaref. Gerlach, Simon, Sherrod and Krupnik, along with Gideon Barr and his wife, Fannie, Jeanne Schaaf, Anne Worthington, Peter Richter, a National Park Service surveyor, and Steve Peterson and Jim Creech, historic architects from the National Park Service, traveled to Ublasaun, the winter village, to collect additional oral and ethnographic data about site use, to study historic Native architecture, and to complete a contour map of Ublasaun. During the same period a film crew from the University of Alaska began work that eventually resulted in production of a documentary film about Inupiaq life and Gideon Barr's early years in the Cape Espenberg area of the Seward Peninsula. Ten days of fieldwork is admittedly not much, but they were able to gather basic genealogical data, map the location of structures at Ublasaun, collect data on site structure, and gather limited ethnographic information at the site and in Shishmaref.

In 1992 an archaeological crew of four from the University of Alaska returned to Cape Espenberg for 10 weeks and more detailed archaeological work at Ublasaun, the spring and summer camps, and the reindeer corral. Archaeological excavation being time consuming, and logistics and distances in the arctic restricting what can actually be accomplished during a short summer field season, they still were able to accomplish quite a bit at each site, but not enough to satisfy some of the stated objectives in the original research design about site structure and community organization. While more work clearly remains to be done, they were generally successful in investigating archaeological sites representative of a seasonal round of a reindeer herding family, their relatives, and associates. Many more sites associated with reindeer herding are known than are described in the study, with relevant places that were occupied from about 1890 to 1940 worthy of future research .

Sacrificing the general for the specific, archaeological attention was focused in 1992 on Gideon Barr, his immediate family, and their site and land use in the early twentieth century, after reindeer were introduced. Although the late nineteenth and early twentieth centuries were a time of tremendous change for the Inupiat of northwestern Alaska, it is interesting that almost no serious archaeological attention has been given to the historic period in general, and to the archaeology of reindeer herding in particular.

In order to investigate the Northwest Alaska reindeer herding system in an historical, economic and ecological framework, emphasis was on understanding regional land and site use-patterns, and on the manner in which the reindeer herding and traditional subsistence economies were integrated. The assumption was that those patterns should be reflected in the distribution of sites across the landscape and in the material culture and season and length of occupation of specific settlements. Time depth is derived through use of a variety of sources, including published and unpublished documentary, oral, and archaeological data collection.

In combination with other data sets, historical archaeology provides a window into material conditions of life and about the organization of settlements and communities, but interpretations of the general pattern are limited by virtue of the fact that our field investigations were intensive rather than extensive. In short, while we can provide information on the use of four places occupied and used by early twentieth century reindeer herders in some detail, there is little to say about stability and change for the entire land-use system.

The history and nature of the reindeer economy and industry in northwestern Alaska has been previously studied in considerable detail using documentary and ethnohistorical sources. Much of this has been oriented specifically toward analysis of the economic decline of the industry in the past and toward the problems and prospects of the future of the industry.

Our study departs from that orientation by focusing on individual herders and their families, how herding was integrated with the subsistence economy, and on how this economic system was expressed in a subsistence and settlement system, with specific archaeological site locations as primary indicators. For the first time, intra-site archaeological investigations of typical material culture, the spatial arrangement of features, and the location of activity areas in reindeer herding sites from the late nineteenth and early twentieth centuries have been undertaken. Our study is also unique in that it's an attempt to use oral history and ethnographic information about periods of site abandonment, decisions about site selection, occupation and abandonment, length of time that houses were occupied and re-used, the number of houses occupied simultaneously, or about the technology and material culture associated with reindeer herding and other subsistence activities in northwestern Alaska.

The entire study, Historical Archaeology and the Early Twentieth Century Reindeer Herding Frontier on the Northern Seward Peninsula, Alaska, is now being prepared for separate publication and was conducted under the auspices of the One Man's Heritage Project of the Shared Beringian Heritage Program, a multidisciplinary collaboration between the University of Alaska Fairbanks and the National Park Service. In its pages we hope that archaeologists, historians, and the descendants of the first northwest Alaskan reindeer herders will find something of interest.

~ S. Craig Gerlach

REFERENCES CITED

Bockstoce, John R.
1986   *Whales, Ice, and Men. The History of Whaling in the Western Arctic.* University of Washington Press.

Fortuine, Robert
1992   *Chills and Fever, Health and Disease in the Early History of Alaska.* University of Alaska Press. Fairbanks.

Jordan, Terry
1993   *North American Cattle Ranching Frontiers, Origins, Diffusion, and Differentiation.* University of New Mexico Press. Albuquerque.

Stern, Richard O., Edward Arobio, Larry L. Naylor, and Wayne C. Thomas
1980   *Eskimos, Reindeer, and Land.* Agricultural Experiment Station, School of Agriculture and Land Resources Management, Bulletin 59. University of Alaska Fairbanks.

Turner, Frederick Jackson
1921   *The Frontier in American History.* New York: H. Holt and Company.

Worster, Donald
1994   *An Unsettled Country, Changing Landscapes of the American West.* University of New Mexico Press. Albuquerque.

Well-established trading networks linked the people of Northwest Alaska with the people of Siberia. According to Moses' legend on the back of the art work, these East Cape [Siberian] Eskimo traders were on their way to Kotzebue in a "big skin boat and whaling boat."
~ By James Kivetoruk Moses.
~ Photo by Trevor Roehl, courtesy of the Alaska State Museum (VA-539).

Gideon Barr remembers that sled deer were used in pairs to make faster and longer trips to distant settlements to trade; but they took longer to train than sled dogs, and on ice "they're real helpless, the hooves always slip so easy."
~ By James Kivetoruk Moses, photo by Trevor Roehl, courtesy of the Alaska State Museum (VA-547).

Archaeologists carefully removed the windblown sand that had buried Makaiqtaq Barr's home and recorded the house as it was left after abandonment. To enter the house, one would enter a stormroom where reindeer equipment such as harness parts, leather straps, and reindeer bells were stored. Sled parts and trapping and hide preparation equipment were also stored here. The cool temperatures of the stormroom also kept seal and reindeer meat fresh. To enter the main living room, one would pass through a short, narrow and low entrance tunnel, constructed to trap cold air and keep drafts out of the house. Inside the main room of the house was a pantry, where items of both European and Native manufacture were found. ~~ Photo by James Simon, 1992.

(Opposite page) University of Alaska Fairbanks archaeologists Jim Simon (center) and Catherine Williams (left) with assistance from Paul Nayokpuk (foreground) began the first in-depth archaeological study of early twentieth century reindeer herding with excavations of Makaiqtaq Barr's home at Ublasaun, 1992. ~~ Photographer unidentified.

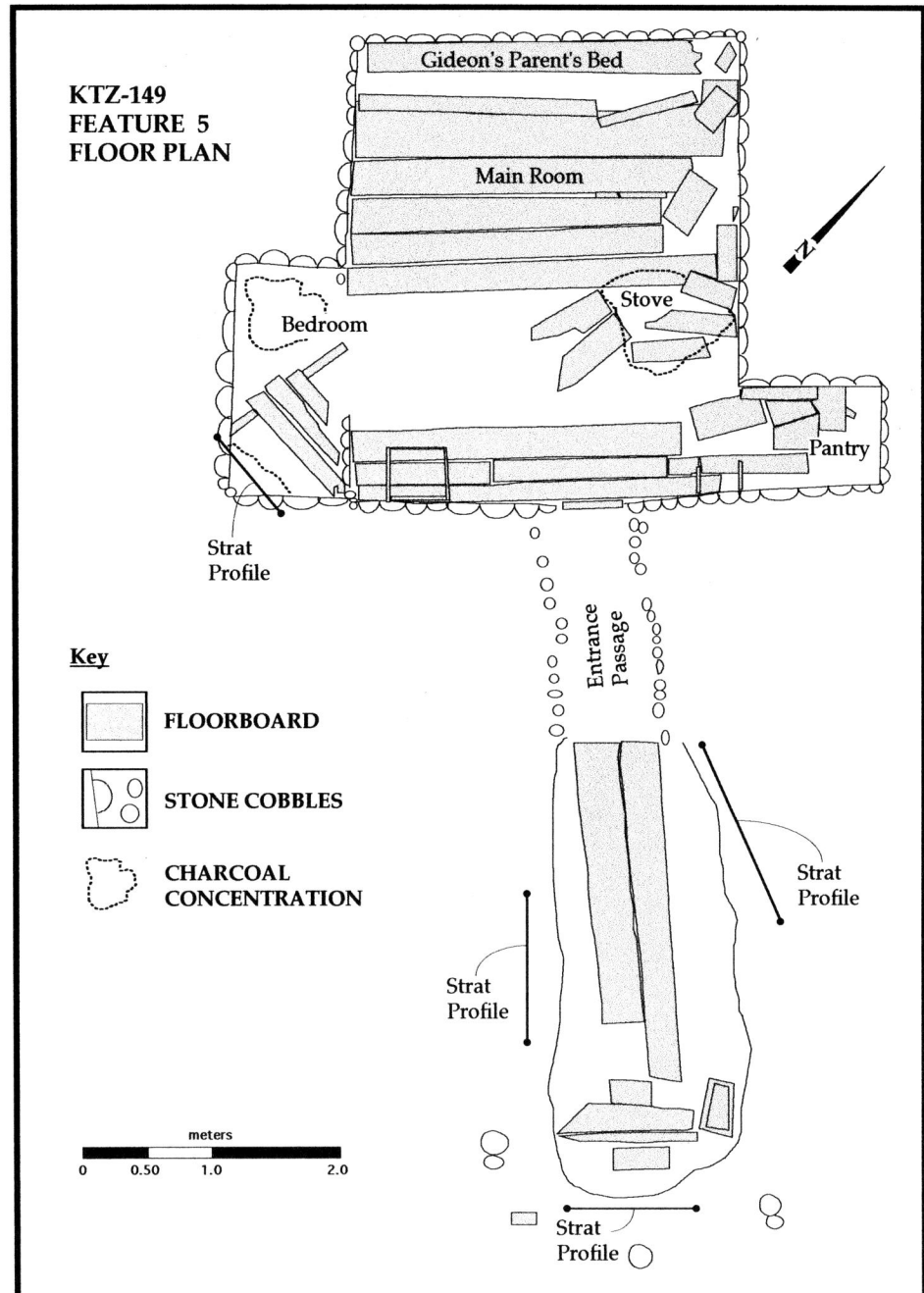

The floor plan of Makaiqtaq Barr's home (Feature 5) at Ublasaun (KTZ-149) as recorded by archaeologists from the University of Alaska Fairbanks, under the overall direction of S. Craig Gerlach and the field direction of James Simon.
~~ Drafted by Ronald Navarro.

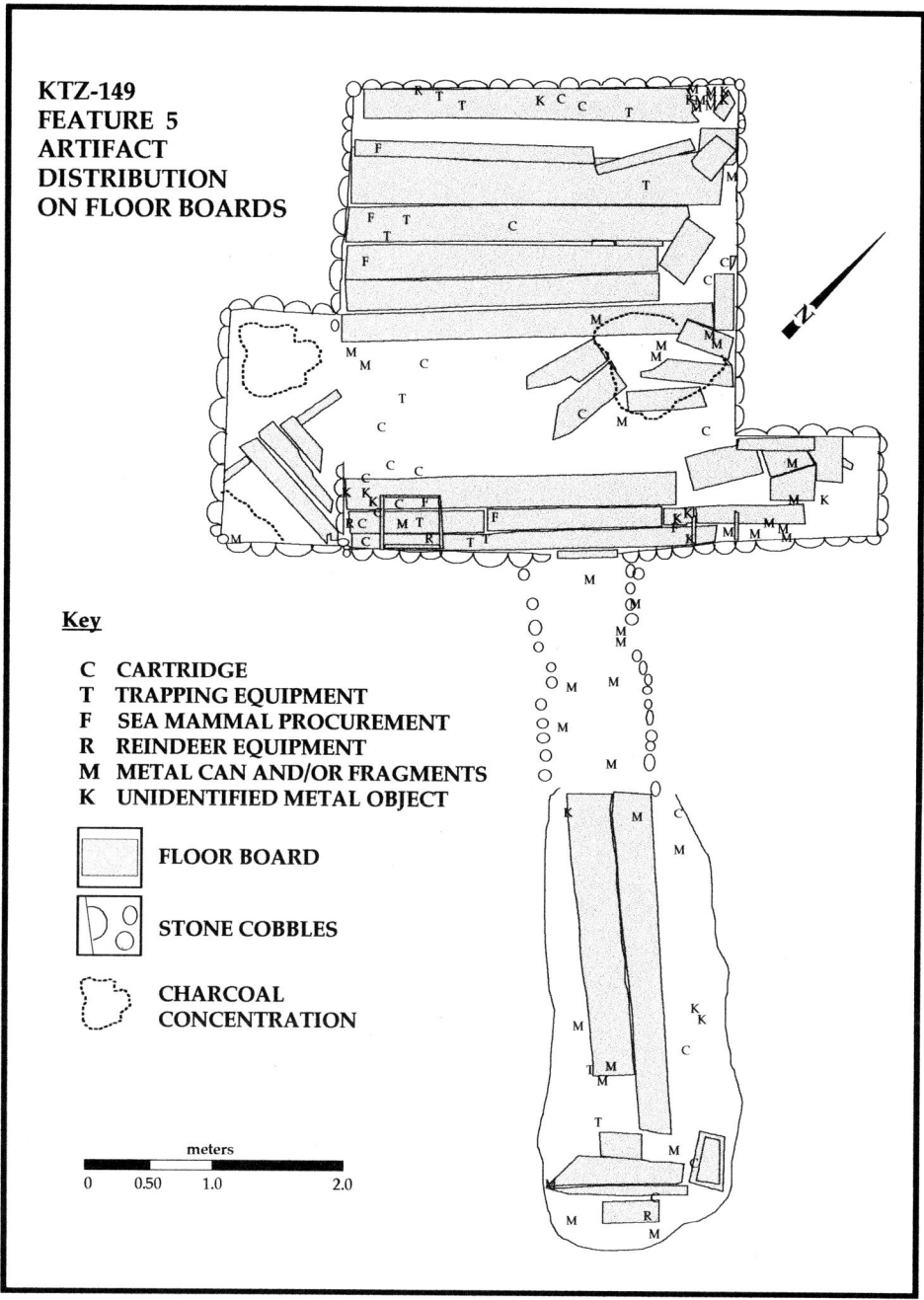

This drawing shows the distribution of artifacts found by archaeologists on the floor boards of Makaiqtaq Barr's home at Ublasaun, 1992. This is one of several maps of the artifact and bone distribution on this house floor. When excavating any site, the archaeologist proceeds with care, making sure to find, map, record, and photograph every artifact and feature. Because excavations effectively destroy the integrity of a site, great care is taken to record the location of every artifact, bone, and feature so that archaeologists are able to "put the site back together" in the laboratory.
~ Drafted by Ronald Navarro.

Historical archaeological investigations were also conducted at a reindeer corral on Cape Espenberg, constructed and used by the Barr family and other herders from 1919 to 1930. The corral was used in the summer when reindeer needed to be handled for removing antlers, castrating, or simply counting heads. The structural remains of the corral and surface artifacts, such as bone and metal cans, were mapped and described by the archaeologists. In this photograph, the archaeologists are excavating a large area to define areas where butchering, skinning, and cooking took place. ~~ Photo by James Simon, 1992.

Summer handlings were major social events. Many people from nearby villages traveled to the corral to help perform all of the tasks during the handlings, which could take several days. Although tiring, reindeer handlings were and still are places where people gather to share food and stories and enjoy the excitement of handling the animals day and night. Top: young men and boys wrestle a reindeer at a handling near Shishmaref. Bottom: children at a large handling near Shishmaref.
~~ Photos by Edward Keithahn, circa 1923, courtesy of Richard Keithahn and National Park Service (neg. 114 and 125).

A detail etched on a late nineteenth century ivory pipe shows an Inupiaq man lassoing a spotted reindeer. Reindeer roundup, marking, and castration was a rough-and-tumble job. Spotted reindeer were particularly prized for their hides, which were used for parkas and are frequently pictured being worn by wealthy young women from Wales. Before reindeer introduction in Northwest Alaska, spotted hides were traded from Siberian herders. ~ Chris Arend photo courtesy of the Anchorage Museum of History and Art (81.58).

Surface historical archaeological investigations at the Espenberg corral uncovered detailed information about how the reindeer were handled. More than 10,000 bones were recovered and analyzed in the study. It is interesting that at this corral, many such entire reindeer skeletons were found. They were not butchered and may represent deer that simply died there, perhaps related to stress from severe winter icing in the mid 1930s.
~~ Photo by James Simon, 1992.

Paul Nayokpuk (right) from Shishmaref and archaeologist Alexander Orekov from Magadan assisted in the excavations of Makaiqtaq Barr's house at Ublasaun in 1992. Local Native participation in the study was important both for the inclusion of indigenous knowledge about the history and ecology of reindeer herding and also for training in the methods and techniques of archaeology. Alexander Orekov is an expert on late prehistoric coastal adaptations in Chukotka and was the first Russian archaeologist to work in the Bering Land Bridge National Preserve. ~~ Photo by James Simon.

Co-researcher Gideon K. Barr Sr. (right) tirelessly shares his knowledge and detailed memory with archaeologist S. Craig Gerlach (left), who directed the historical archaeology studies of early twentieth century reindeer herding, and NPS archaeologist Jeanne Schaaf, Espenberg 1991.
~~ Photo by James Simon.

Tales and Places, Toponyms and Heroes

*It's no longer a river anymore in
these days.
So, it's just an old site
-- which becomes just a story.*

~ Gideon Kahlook Barr Sr.

(Opposite page)
Qipalut, or Cape Deceit, near Deering, located on the south shore of Kotzebue Sound, June 1995. ~ Photo by Jeanne Schaaf.

Ties between place, place-names, and the verbal arts form an integral part of the lives of Inupiaq residents of Northwest Alaska. Those who know the coastline between Ikpik, Shishmaref, Qivaluaq, Ikpizaaq, Cape Espenberg, and settlements beyond: Nuwianii, Taugaaluuvik, Ipnatchiaq (now Deering,) read the land as a text, retelling what it knows--and how they and their ancestors have experienced it--as they drive their boats to spring ugruk hunting sites, settle into opulent spots to pick salmonberries, fish for tomcods, and engage in the multitude of subsistence tasks that keep them whole. Toponyms, names of places, are cultural artifacts, to be certain, but they are also vehicle and symbol of cultural ideology. The reading of the land is personal--often it relates to the history and genealogy of a particular teller--and it is communal; many of the tales told define what it is to be Tapqaamiut, the people of the sandy shore, and name where that identity is centered.

First, the bonds of family and sense of community are intensely important to the Inupiat of this region. Tied closely to all-important kinship is a vast network of sharing, whether it be of food, stories, cash, or shelter. And in order to survive and share, one must live from and know the land. Place thus becomes the core of what must be known in order to prosper. Land, for the Inupiat, is an entity much like a person. From this viewpoint, the earth itself can speak, and one of the ways it has spoken and continues to narrate Inupiaq experience and worldview is through the placement and transmission of names. There are a number of tales from this region that refer to persons actually traveling through or being within the land, rather than existing upon it, as Westerners do. This kind of situation occurred at Serpentine Hot Springs (Iyat, meaning cooking pot) where shamanistic initiation took place through underground travel in several layers of permafrost. The earth became, for a shaman's sometimes unwilling apprentices, both opponent and mentor during these experiences. Certain places are still "quoted," as though they can talk. Gideon Barr Sr., says of the place Agugvik ("to put a skirt on" or "root place") "it acts the same as Ipnauraq (Arctic River locality), but not very many people go there" (Barr 1988).

Hattie Ningeulook, a Shishmaref elder, historian, and skinsewer, now deceased, once framed a tale she told her son Edgar by saying, "They say that in those days past, the earth possesses them" (H. Ningeulook 1982). What did Hattie Ningeulook mean by this? If "the river acts" and "the earth possesses" these Inupiaq people, arriving at truths about the relationship of the Kigiqtaamiut (people of Shishmaref) with all that surrounds them may be very difficult for an outsider, perhaps even for a local person. Taken literally, did Ningeulook's words mean that people here cannot be separated from the earth without giving up their identity? Is such an identity individual, communal, or something else altogether? When the ancestors of a people have lived in a region for centuries, the history of that region and the names of its places have passed verbally from storyteller to student, from parent to child, what is the "attachment" that is experienced, the history that becomes known, the feelings that are felt? What are the processes by which naming, knowing, and conducting lives happen? Does Ningeulook's statement imply that the earth not only compels, but controls people in their destinies? Certainly, land, sea, and the presence of game shape human actions from a subsistence standpoint. The commonly told personal narratives of survival also indicate that individual character and Inupiaq worldview are consistently molded from encounters with earth and weather.

The stories of the ancestors and the place-names themselves tell how, in the moral and practical sense, to be Inupiat. Some tales underscore Inupiaq ties with earth and destiny; they provide predictive models of what is like to be a person from this region. One of the sites best known to non-Natives in this area lies in the uplands. Serpentine Hot Springs, or Iyat, is surrounded by granite tors, some that were transformed from women to stone. The site has been used for traditional healing for generations. A well-known tradition associated with Iyat was the practice of dipping mukluk ties in the hot springs water to predict their wearer's life span. If the strings curled up, the life of the wearer was predicted to be short; and, often, say area residents, that was the case.

Toponyms are both functionally and artistically imbedded in Tapqaamiut life. The patterns associated with place-naming here are expressive and affiliated closely with the following themes: geography (the lay of the land), subsistence use of land and sea, kinship and social structure, local history, and Inupiaq beliefs. In order to read the land, one must know the names it has been assigned and the information associated with those names. The tales interwined with the names comprise a part of the "folk literature" of this region, one that is highly variable in "form, origin, and function" (Degh 1989 [1969]:121).

The place-name classifications proposed in this essay are patterns revealed in collecting toponyms and tales from several key collaborators in Northwest Alaska. They are not, at this point, classifications recognized by the Inupiat themselves, but are working definitions. Only further research will disclose local structures and genres of place-names and determine how the remembering, forgetting, and invention of toponyms works.

It is useful to know the descriptive or geographic toponyms associated entirely with features of this landscape. One might think they would be the most commonplace toponyms, but that may not be the case. There are a number of generic descriptive toponyms that are common, however, describing areas like portages, mud flats, and islands. Some of these generic toponyms are very useful in assessing potentially dangerous situations, while others may lead astray a traveler who is unfamiliar with the local dialect. Such a term is saniniq itself. According to Edgar Ningeulook of Shishmaref, along the Tapqaq coast, saniniq (meaning land between two points) refers to a particular sandy beach. However, the long expanse of coastline from Cape Espenberg to Deering is also called saniniq; and in the Pitagmiut dialect, the term means shallow ocean, indicating that the area must be known well and traveled with care (Barr 1991; Burch 1991). Closely related to the descriptive toponym is the place-name associated with an activity conducted at a particular site. While this type of toponym may reflect either geography, activity, or both, what it means to a local person is the performance of an activity (most often a subsistence activity,) a historic event associated with the site, or both. This might be called an activity toponym. Some activity toponyms are tied to festivals, trading, athletic competitions, and other social events or cultural activities. Ublasaun, or "first light," was a site that served as a reindeer camp and eventually attracted many members of the extended family of Makaiqtaq and Emily Barr, who helped with the herding. The place-name refers to the fact that this was a prime seal netting location and early risers, mostly young boys, were able to engage in "finders-keepers" when they found seals lost from the nets the previous night. They took the animals home to their families, thus sharing in subsistence responsibilities.

Both geographic place-names and activity toponyms are closely associated with Inupiaq national and family structure in the telling. Their allocation and transmission are very careful processes that bolster extended family and community solidarity by establishing territories and recording important events in family, local, and regional Inupiaq history. Toponyms are cultural artifacts; but they don't just turn up on the land as descriptions and so, should not be collected and recorded simply as "things."

At the extended family level, toponyms and associated tales once served to deliniate language boundaries and perhaps to demarcate lands over which skirmishes might be fought. Within the local family, tales were (and still are) told by individuals about their ancestral lands, tying a kin group to a certain place and to its heroes, heroines, birthrights, and times of struggle. I call toponyms of this type family texts that most often are personal narratives. Many times they tell tales of individual survival, either of the person telling the story or of one of his or her ancestors. Often, they are told with a certain amount of irony, as the struggle to live is well known to all. Generally, these stories are unknown to other families unless they are performed publicly (say, at an Elders' Conference) or have been written down.

Like geographic toponyms and activity names, only a few family texts have singular reference and meaning. Many simultaneously mean activity, geography, family, nation, or historical event. On the Saniniq coast, Taugaaluuvik was located at the outlet of Sullivan Creek (Burch 1994:394, 410; Ray 1983:217/71). Gideon Barr Sr. tells a lengthy tale about the hero Ilaganiq to emphasize a portage (itivliq) needed to avoid the beast, for Taugaaluuvik was known for "enveloping whole objects... [like] a fully loaded umiaq" (Barr 1991). The story provides an excellent example of how a place-name, a geographic feature (the sea cove where Taugaaluuvik lived,) a community, a creature, a tale, and a message of avoidance can be intertwined.

Because many actual sites, both ancient and historic, are now abandoned or have eroded completely away into the sea, tales associated with them sometimes substitute for the place itself. Thus, the toponym remains alive and closely associated with Inupiaq morals and beliefs. These remembered toponyms I call memory names, because the place itself may no longer exist. "I feel like she is really still there and a part of me when I think of the stories she used to tell," says folklorist Sandra Dolby Stahl about her grandmother. "In fact, these stories are perhaps the more precious reminders, since they scarcely have an existence outside my memory" (1989:ix). Jack Herman Ningeulook once told the tale of a leader, Atturaq, whose people found a large baleen whale stranded at the community there (1984). The meat was inedible, but they wanted the baleen, so Atturaq ordered a diver to go underwater and tie the fronds together. Then, all the people of Tuqsrugnak pulled the baleen out together. The community effort convinced the chief, who was entitled to half the take, that all members should share the other half equally, although he had promised it to the diver. The diver became angry and attacked the chief, a transgression that banished the man from the village and allowed his return only after an appropriate time. Thus, the memory name Tuqsrugnak signifies community effort, appropriate sharing, and proper respect for leadership for Tapqaamiut today.

The tales associated with toponyms that bolster national identity are creation tales and the stories of legendary heroes, like the tale of Ilaganiq, which follows. They are sometimes also stories of intersocietal and intercontinental wars. These names and their stories are mnemonics, or memory devices, for defining particular territories. The lines here between myth (the story of how we came to be as a people or how this land was formed) and legend (the historicity of an event) are often blurred.

The story of Ilaganiq -- told by former Cape Espenberg residents as well as Buckland and Deering peoples -- emphasizes national identity. As told by Gideon Barr Sr., however, the tale is one of a legendary strongman thought to have been related to the Barr family far back in time. The actual genealogy can no longer be traced. Ilaganiq's siblings migrated elsewhere; but Ilaganiq, remaining at home, continued to provide for his sister and mother, even after his sister relocated to Cape Krusenstern. In order to take food to her, he hunted large whales (which is unusual for this area,) and, being a strongman, swam the food across the sound. But Ilaganiq became too forceful to fit in with his people and began to terrorize area hunters. On trips north, he forced men time and again to give up all their hard won caribou skins -- Barr refers to these hunters as "slaves." They finally ended their subservience by stuffing Ilaganiq and his skins into his kayak so tightly that he couldn't maneuver, then killing him with bows and arrows as he paddled from shore.

When Ilaganiq's mother heard of her son's death, she became so angry that she took her mitten and reshaped the entire cape, making the waters so treacherous and the shoals so shallow that hunters from elsewhere would no longer be successful there (Barr 1987). A large whale skull marking the Ilaganiq site has been moved by Barr ancestors before it, too, is lost to the relentless ocean, much as a curator maintains an important artifact or collection. Thus, the mythological aspect of the tale ties creation of their land and to a powerful Inupiaq heroine. The legendary components of place-names on the cape refer to Ilaganiq, who is at once strongman (an admirable Inupiaq man), hero (one who can support many), and badman (one who does not share). The message of the tale to today's listeners is to emulate Ilaganiq's good qualities and powerful traits while bearing in mind the not-so-admirable faults that caused his death.

My thanks extend to Edgar Nuna Ningeulook, Gideon K. Barr Sr., Fannie Barr, and Harvey Pootoogooluk. Larry Kaplan assisted with the Inupiaq orthography. Ernest S. Burch Jr. and Dorothy Jean Ray stand in the foreground of any work on Northwest Alaska. *Quyana.*

~ Susan W. Fair

Shishmaref elder, Harvey Pootoogooluk, August 1993. ~ Photo by James Magdanz.

SOURCES

Barr, Gideon K. Sr.
1991 Tape-recorded interview (audiotape) by Ernest S. Burch Jr. and Igor Krupnik; transcribed by Michael Faugno, 11 July 1991. Shishmaref, AK. U.S. National Park Service, Alaska System Support Office. Shared Beringian Heritage Program, Anchorage, AK.

1988 *Gideon Barr's Place-Names.* Bureau of Indian Affairs Interview, 88-ESP-005 to 88-ESP-011. Self- audiotaped interview conducted by Barr. Shishmaref, AK.

1987 Tape-recorded interview (audiotape) by Jeanne Schaaf, 15-16 May 1987. Nome, AK.

Burch, Ernest S. Jr.
1994 *The Cultural and Natural Heritage of Northwest Alaska.* Vol. V. The Inupiaq Nations of Northwest Alaska. Kotzebue, AK: NANA Museum of the Arctic and Anchorage, AK: U.S. National Park Service, Alaska System Support Office.

1991 Unpublished working notes, "Place-Name data from Gideon Barr," 11 July 1991.

Degh, Linda
1989[1969] *Folktales & Society: Storytelling in a Hungarian Peasant Community.* Bloomington: Indian University Press, trans. by Emily M. Schossberger.

Fair, Susan W. and Edgar N. Ningeulook
1995 *Qamani: Up the Coast in My Mind, in My Heart.* Manuscript on file, National Park Service, Anchorage, AK.

Ningeulook, Hattie
1982 Tape-recorded interview (audiotape) with Edgar Ningeulook, translated and transcribed by Edgar Ningeulook, 15-16 June 1982. Edgar Ningeulook, Shishmaref, AK.

Ningeulook, Jack Herman
1984 Tape-recorded interview (audiotape) with Edgar Ningeulook, translated and transcribed by Edgar Ningeulook, February 1984. Shishmaref, AK. Eskimo Heritage Project, SH/EN-84 Nome, AK: Kawerak, Inc.

Stahl, Sandra Dolby
1989 *Literary Folkloristics and the Personal Narrative.* Bloomington: Indiana University Press.

***

A hunter camouflaged in a white cotton drill parka stalks a basking seal with a seal scratcher. When he is close to the lead, he will harpoon the animal, then haul it home for his wife to butcher, and share it.
~ James Kivetoruk Moses, circa 1960s, watercolor, colored pencil, India ink.
   Photo by Trevor Roehl, courtesy of the Alaska State Museum (VA-966).

William Allockeok (Allagiaq) sits at Iyat (Serpentine Hot Springs), the hot springs on the uplands of the Serpentine River. Allagiaq wears a fur headband and waterproof boots. The springs have been a sacred area and a center of healing for centuries. The area, in a valley framed by dramatic granite tors, was also used in the past for shamanistic initiation. Today, the National Park Service maintains a community bath and bunkhouse at the site, which has become a popular recreation destination for those who fly small aircraft and for villagers, who travel there by snowmachine and dog team in March and April when the daylight hours are long.
~~ Photo by Edward Keithahn, circa 1923, courtesy of Richard Keithahn and National Park Service (neg. 005).

William Allockeok's (Allagiaq) daughter, Elsie Weyiouanna visited Iyat (Serpentine Hot Springs) in 1995 and remembered many stories about her family's camps there when she was small. She recalled, in Inupiaq, stories about the powerful shamans who resided there. Some of the striking granite tors surrounding the hot springs are shown in the background. Folktales commemorate women who were turned to stone and are seated there now as tors.
~ Photo by Jeanne Schaaf.

Traditional city councils were a powerful force in traditional village life, exercising judgments regarding marital difficulties, land disputes, and conflicts with other groups. This photo includes (from left) Johnny Weyiouanna, Washington Kapikzruaq, an unidentified child, George Olanna of Ikpik, Minnie Olanna with Ida Olanna, Saavgaq, Leona Cross (Mizugnaat), Mary and Joseph Eningowuk and a child, and Taqtu. Known council members who saved the village of Shishmaref from disaster and who are in this photo include Kapikzruaq, George Olanna of Ikpik, Mizugnaat, who was also a midwife and healer, and Taqtu. Kapikzruaq and Taqtu had been practicing shamans.
~~ Photo by Edward Keithahn, circa 1923, courtesy of Richard Keithahn and National Park Service (neg. 047).

Harry Kigrook, father of Fannie Barr, poses with Beulah Palaktaq Okonok and her son Harry. Beulah was the sister of shaman and storyteller Washington Kapikzruaq's wife. She and her husband William raised Shishmaref sculptor Harvey Pootoogooluk at Qivaluaq, an isolated location north of Shishmaref along the coast after their son Harry's death.
~~ Photo by Edward Keithahn, circa 1923, courtesy of Richard Keithahn and National Park Service (neg. 071).

Stephen Igalukviaq, known to villagers as "Grandpa Whiskers," migrated into Shishmaref from unknown regions. He and his elderly wife divided their time between the east and west forks of the Serpentine River. It was said that he "hardly ate fish" because he had to maintain a salt-free diet. Some people today speculate that he came originally from caribou country. Edward Keithahn relates a brief tale about the death of Igalukviaq's wife "Mrs. Whiskers Comes Home" in *Eskimo Adventures: Another Journey into the Primitive* (1923:47-48).

~~ Photo by Edward Keithahn, circa 1923, courtesy of Richard Keithahn and National Park Service (neg. 027).

Looking west over Shishmaref in winter, snow-covered sod houses blend in with the landscape while, the roof of a "lumber house," which belonged to either William Allockeok or Carson Tingook, the Native Store manager, stands out in the distance.
~~ Photo by Edward Keithahn, circa 1923, courtesy of Richard Keithahn and National Park Service (neg. 006).

Tomcod fishing is an important activity in both spring and fall, particularly at certain locations. This woman is preparing a hole for fishing on the lagoon side of Shishmaref. While she is scooping ice out of the hole, she has stood her fishing pole upright in the snow behind her. Her sled is called a basket sled and is smaller for easily pushing or pulling. Ikpizaaq, up the Tapqaq coast from Shishmaref, was a settlement where ugruk hunting was especially productive, where intensive seal netting also took place in the winter under the ice, and where fishing for tomcod, smelt, bullhead, and great schools of cod was also excellent. Seining for tomcod, whitefish, smelt, and grayling at the mouth of the Serpentine River near Ipnauraq was once an activity the Kigiqtaamiut engaged in before the beginning of school in October.

~~ Photo by Edward Keithahn, circa 1923, courtesy of Richard Keithahn and National Park Service (neg. 012).

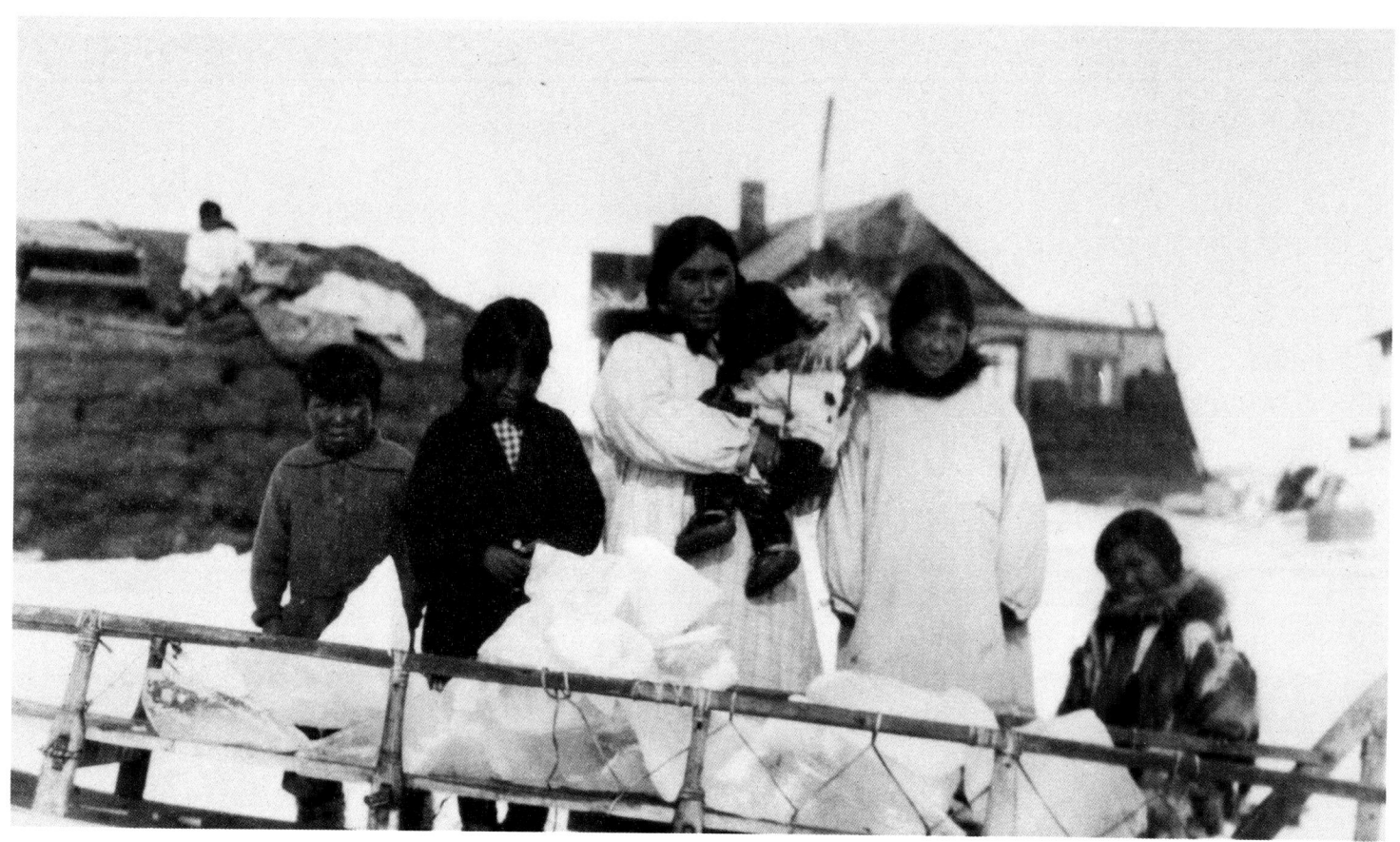

Anna Weyiouanna of Shishmaref, remembered as an excellent skinsewer, poses here with her children Alex, Irene, baby Esau, Nellie, and Bertha (Pootoogooluk) behind Bertha's great-grandmother Myna Eutok's sod house. The freight sled in the foreground is loaded with blocks of ice to be used for drinking water. Shishmaref residents still haul ice and collect rainwater for drinking.
~ Photo by Edward Keithahn, circa 1923, courtesy of Richard Keithahn and National Park Service (neg. 059).

(Opposite page)
The Messenger Feast or Wolf Dance was an important post-subsistence harvesting event. The closest location that it was probably held to Kigiqtaq, Old Shishmaref, was across the lagoon near the Serpentine River mouth, where the beating of drums conveyed the invitation to all who could hear and listeners transmitted the information beyond. Charlie Okpowruk of Shishmaref describes the "invitation dance" as evidenced by the etchings here: *"When they see the ones who they invited, they always go to them running... go meet them, and then those two are cousins. That's a story I have from the old people"* **(Okpowruk 1991).**
~~ By James Kivetoruk Moses, circa 1965.
~~ Photo by Chris Arend, courtesy of the Anchorage Museum of History and Art (70.164.1).

A detail from the top of a walrus ivory pipe carved in Wales before the turn of the century shows two baleen whales, one of which has a human inua, or spirit, or is undergoing some kind of transformation. Transformation is an important part of the Inupiaq belief system, where humans are tied to animals in an endless cycle of subsistence and movement.
~~ Photo by Chris Arend, courtesy of the Anchorage Museum of History and Art (72.66.6).

Tales and Places, Toponyms, and Heroes -- 125

Ilaganiq, a Folktale

*... Long ago, the land had animals
  that are no longer present.
They were large and dangerous.
They were known to kill and endanger the lives
  of human beings who lived in the land.*

~ Gideon K. Barr Sr.

(Opposite page)
Painting by James Kivetoruk Moses.
~ Photo by Trevor Roehl, courtesy of Alaska State Museum (VA-550).

*The place where I will start is an old igloo site
  at Cape Espenberg.
This man's name, Ilaganiq, it's the story.
Just from the story I inherit from my grandparents.*

*His home was right at the tip of Espenberg just a few hundred
  yards away from the lighthouse.
The largest whale what Ilaganiq caught with hunting from a
  qayaq [it is placed there].
That's the largest whale he has bagged.
So he took the head off, and one side of the jawbone, and put it
  on top of the ground—
So his ancestors were able to see
  how big a whale he caught from his own qayaq.
What he made himself for hunting.
And his home is still in the area—
Just few yards away from the whale head right now.*

*There were three brothers and one sister and Ilaganiq's mother.
And when they grew up, they couldn't get along in one home.
So they decided to move out when they become a man,
  and when their sister become a woman.
So Ilaganiq's brother, Kuvravak—
He made a home at Deering, Alaska.
And his other brother doesn't really have a home.
He was a traveler.
It is a long story behind Kuvravak
  when he takes off for inland up Kobuk River way,
And their sister, she decided to reside at Cape Krusenstern.
That's right across from Cape Espenberg,
  just northwest of Kotzebue.
And they all moved out of the one place
  except Ilaganiq and his mother.*

(The story continues narrated in Inupiaq
and translated by Herbert O. Anungazuk.)

... Long ago, the land had animals that are no longer present.
They were large and dangerous.
They were known to kill and endanger the lives of human
*   beings who lived in the land.*

When the children [at Cape Espenberg] matured—
The third child, brother of Ilaganiq, did not wish to establish
*   residence in the village where they lived.*
He told them that he would walk to other lands—
And hunt animals that were known
*   to kill the people of those regions.*

So, because of his personal commitments,
*   he was never in one area too long.*
He went to other places to learn and hear about animals
*   that had threatened the people's safety.*
Ilaganiq (also) earned a reputation of removing
*   dangerous animals that had killed Inupiat in the past.*
He cleared the land of danger
*   making it safe for the people that lived there.*
Whenever Ilaganiq heard of a dangerous animal,
*   he would seek that animal.*
He did not rest until he killed it.

In the waters near Ipnaziaq (Deering)—
Near the cliffs called Taugaaluuvik,
*   there was an animal that lived*
*   in the deep waters there, just offshore.*
This being resembled a huge, tarp-like gelatinous mass
*   capable of enveloping whole objects.*
The creature was known to swallow a fully loaded umiaq
*   and return to the depths intact.*
Its prey was never known to escape.

Ilaganiq heard about this dangerous creature
*   when he went to Ipnaziaq.*
He went to the area soon after hearing about it.
Ilaganiq's decision was immediate, and, very soon,
*   he was in position, after the creature.*
Ilaganiq swam in the waters near the cliffs
*   where the creature was known to be.*
It was not long before he sensed the creature
*   coming out of the depths after him.*

Surely, panic was an ally to the creature.
And for a moment, pure terror gripped Ilaganiq.
The creature wrapped itself around Ilaganiq almost instantly.
But Ilaganiq had time to form himself into a sphere—
So that when he needed to,
*   he could exert all his strength to free himself.*
He can feel the creature tighten his hold around the hunter.
And the hunter felt the creature settle back
*   into the bottom of the sea.*

All movement stopped, and,
*   knife in hand, Ilaganiq sprang into action—*
Tearing himself and exerting all of his strength
*   from the very death-grip that enveloped him.*
Ilaganiq was free and swam slowly toward the light above him.
His action resulted in the death of the creature—
Releasing the waters of further danger to travelers.

The point had a gentle slope into the water
*   near the cliffs—with a saddle not far inland.*
People who traveled near the dangerous waters would land
*   near the cliffs where the creature was known to be.*
They portaged their boat to safer waters on the other side.
If a craft continued around the cape unknowingly,
*   they would fall victim to the creature.*
Those travelers that took the time to portage
*   through the saddle—*
They guaranteed their safety.
They would arrive safely at their destination.

The water is deep at the point—
It is deep.

This creature was named Taugaaluuvik.
This area must have been used to portage boats
for many, many years by many, many people.
There was a deep rut through this place
and there was a gentle slope on both sides of the trail.
This change in the land
occurred through constant use of many boats
being taken through there for many years.

It is true.
Ilaganiq had torn the vitals of the creature
in his escape from its grasp.
This killed the creature—
Ridding the area of danger to travelers in the offshore waters...
Ilaganiq successfully killed the creature.

Ilaganiq decided not to continue his travel
by qayaq any farther.
The fall season was just days away when he began his travel.
And he decided he would continue overland.
As was customary for him when he walked,
he dragged a baleen sled behind him.

Ilaganiq began his travels in a place called Kaniq (Buckland).
In continuing his travels, he encountered some people
just south of the Kobuk River not far from its mouth.
He arrived at the camp bearing the survival equipment
he carried in his sled—
But he left his provisions there,
just out of sight from the small village.
Ilaganiq stopped and stayed with the family.
There was a total of four people in the house.
The couple he encountered were elderly.
The mother of the elderly man's wife was living with them.
The fourth person was the daughter of the elderly couple
who had just reached maturity and was very young.

Ilaganiq married the young woman,
who soon bore him a son.
The family ate very little at mealtime, and soon,
Ilaganiq knew he would need far more nourishment
than what he got eating their meals.
The pangs of hunger won—
Ilaganiq returned secretly to the provisions
he had stored with his sled to supplement his diet.
Ilaganiq pondered for many days,
but his final decision was to leave the family.
This was based purely on the desire to survive.
He was constantly hungry,
and he knew his body needed far more nutrition
than what he was getting with the family.
He hunted and provided—
But always, the portions at mealtime were small.

Ilaganiq left the family not long after the birth of his son.
Ilaganiq walked along the banks of the river
and decided after a short while
that he must construct a craft to speed up his travel.
He decided he would build a qayaq.
And he gathered the material he would need for construction.
In the deepening dusk, he completed his task
and piled up the wood and the bark he would use.
Tomorrow he would begin its construction.
And he prepared his bed away from the immediate area.
Very soon he was asleep, and he slept undisturbed
throughout the evening.

Ilaganiq awoke to the sound of voices.
He heard many different tones,
but was unable to understand all he could hear.
He listened, unmoving, and peered toward the voices
with squinted eyes, feigning sleep.
The voices were animals talking amid themselves.
All were around the pile of wood and bark
that Ilaganiq had put together to build his qayaq.
Ilaganiq can hear that they were conferring

about what the pile was for.
They decided that the sleeping man
    had put the material together to construct a boat.

From where Ilaganiq lay,
    he saw two sandhill cranes, a pair of ptarmigan,
    and an arctic hare.
A porcupine was also among them.
There were other animals that were around the pile
    that the hunter could not see.
But by the sounds of their voices he can make out
    what type of animal they were.
They were all discussing what each piece was for,
    and they proceed to start in the building of the qayaq.

All the animals worked as one in construction of the qayaq—
Very soon, the frame was completed.
The resin from surrounding trees was used
    to seal the seams as the wood bark was being sewn on.
A pair of porcupines, (because of their prowess in working
    with wood)
Smeared the pitch onto the seams, making the vessel
    waterproof.

Ilaganiq watched the boat-building process,
    feigning sleep, during the whole time unmoving.
The hunter was very impressed with the speed
    that the animals showed in the building of the boat.
Ilaganiq knew it would have taken him a few days
    to complete it if he had constructed it himself.
He was in awe that it took them just part of the day
    to complete its construction.
The animals left the site as soon as they finished the craft.

As soon as Ilaganiq saw that the last of the animals had left,
    he rose from his bed and ate breakfast.
Soon, he tested the seaworthiness of the qayaq,
    which the animals had recently completed for him.
His qayaq glided smoothly downriver.

Ilaganiq rarely dipped his paddle into the water
    as the current carried him downstream.
Ilaganiq saw many animals as he slowly drifted—
He knew from stories told that some animals that are now
    present were not present there at earlier times.
The lower estuaries of the Kobuk river,
    [for example], did not support the lynx,
    according to the many stories he had heard.
The river system did not have an arctic hare
    that provided for the subsistence of the lynx.

As Ilaganiq continued, he encountered a person
    sitting on the banks of the Kobuk.
The hunter stopped and asked questions
    that would assist him in his travels.
This done, the person asked Ilaganiq if he
    could accompany him.
Ilaganiq put the person on board his qayaq—
But the craft was too small to safely carry
    more than one person on board.
His passenger was just too heavy.
After an attempt to carry his passenger,
    Ilaganiq decided that they must get to shore
    so that the load can be lightened.
His passenger did not carry anything
    of material value with him.
And Ilaganiq pondered on what to remove
    to lighten the load of his passenger.
The only option he saw was to physically remove something
    directly from his passenger.
Ilaganiq did this by surgically removing
    the entire small intestines of his passenger.
The hunter made the reconnection by sewing the man
    together—
He caused the wound to heal very quickly.

As soon as this was done, Ilaganiq's passenger stated that his
    weight was indeed lessened.
The passenger, Ilaganiq knew, to be a part of the lynx family

in human form...
They continued on until his passenger decided
to cease travel not far from the river's mouth.
Ilaganiq landed his craft on the banks and let him off.
He cast off immediately, eager to continue.
Ilaganiq traveled further downstream alone,
relieved of the excess weight he had removed.
He traveled at leisurely speed absorbing the scenery
and savoring the natural smell of the river.

As Ilaganiq rounded the next bend in the river,
he encountered another person.
Ilaganiq could see that the person was of small stature.
And even before the hunter landed,
he was asked if he could accompany him
on the rest of the travel.
Ilaganiq did not relent, and granted his permission
to accompany him even before he knew who or what
this person was.
Among Ilaganiq's equipment was a throwing board.
The hunter instructed the man on the beach after he had landed
to change the implement into a qayaq.
The man did so, and the qayaq was of perfect size
for his small stature.
Ilaganiq launched his craft again and let the river
determine their speed.

Not long into the start of their trip, his companion began to ask
Ilaganiq if he would land for a short while.
The hunter was usually asked as they encountered a riverbend,
with willow branches dipping into the water.
On landing, the person would go into the willows
and return, chewing something that Ilaganiq
could not really see.

Ilaganiq grew tired of his new companion's constant landing.
It was delaying his travel.
The hunter began to show his discontent on his
companion's actions.

He insisted that the man leave his company.
When the man returned to the craft again after landing,
Ilaganiq stated to the man behind him:
"Let your qayaq become what it was."
Immediately after, Ilaganiq heard water thrashing behind him.
The hunter turned his craft around and saw
that the qayaq had returned to its original form,
casting its passenger into the water.

The person was nowhere to be seen—
But Ilaganiq saw an arctic hare that was showing
extreme difficulty in returning to the safety
of the banks of the river.
To Ilaganiq, the arctic hare did not know how to swim,
but somehow made the river bank in safety.
He retrieved the throwing board
that was floating just in front of him,
and continued on his way.
The estuaries of the Kobuk River
did not have many willows near its banks,
according to the old stories.
But their steady growth increased after their use as food—
By the passenger of Ilaganiq's who in reality
was an arctic hare...

(The story continues after a short break.)

[Ilaganiq proceeds to go caribou hunting].
In the land across the Cape, caribou often spend the summers
feeding near the coast on plants that grow
wild in the land.
The people hunted the caribou there
while they have their summer coats...
These are ideal for parkas (while the hair is not thick).
They use the skins of young caribou and fawns born that
spring because of their durability.
They also used them for their bedding.

Ilaganiq used to visit the hunters with his qayaq

*when he thought that the hunters
    would be successful in their hunts...*
Before the hunters returned to their homes
    from the hunts after spending the summer
    hunting caribou on the mainland.
Ilaganiq's habit was that he would browse
    through the caribou skins of the hunters.
He would take what he needed without asking for them.
The hunters disliked the way he did this,
    but were in no position to take care of it alone.
They would have to deal with the problem as one.
Ilaganiq was a big man.

After obtaining what he needed for himself and his mother,
    Ilaganiq would return home.
One group of Natinnaamiut hunters
    did not approve at all of Ilaganiq's habit.
They devised a plan to rid themselves of him,
    as they now considered Ilaganiq a hindrance.
To them, his actions did not grant forgiveness from the people.
The plan was to cram Ilaganiq's qayaq with additional skins—
After Ilaganiq had placed the skins he took from them
    inside his qayaq before heading home.
This plan would severely restrict Ilaganiq
    from any avenues of swift escape when the measure
    to execute him was carried out by those given
    the grim task.

The Natinnaamiut had devised the plan days before.
They knew that Ilaganiq would raid their store,
    as was now his custom.
Rarely were the hunters successful to excess
    in their quest to obtain adequate numbers
    of caribou hides for their parkas and bedding.
What Ilaganiq was doing interfered with their very survival.
Their main concern was having enough skins
    for their women and children.

The Natinnaamiut expected Ilaganiq, and he came.

The hunters came with many more skins—
They proceeded as planned.
Ilaganiq felt the snugness of the skins around him
    and knew that he might be in extreme danger.
He could not make a swift exit from his qayaq without first
    removing the hides that were placed around him.
On the completion of their task—
The hunters retreated from the qayaq.
Ilaganiq realized that something was amiss
    and asked them as they departed:
        "What are you doing to me?"
He asked them again and did not receive a response
    to his question.
"We will help you cast off," was the only answer he got from
    the group that had crammed his qayaq
    with the caribou hides.

Ilaganiq did not know that just out of his sight—
Archers were preparing the final phase of their plan.
The chosen [assassins] had armed themselves
    with bows and arrows.
They were prepared to shoot their arrows into Ilaganiq,
    should he show them signs of retaliation.
The archers emerged using shields of discarded skin tents
    for protection—
In the event that their adversary should take
    protective measures in defending himself.
When Ilaganiq fully realized that his life was in danger,
    he retaliated by fiercely lashing out his paddle
    at the men around him.
His inability to defend himself properly
    was due to what the men had done.
The caribou hides impeded all crucial movement.
Immediately, Ilaganiq's action resulted in the deaths
    of two in the group.
Ilaganiq had delivered a swift glancing blow
    which killed them instantly.
But an arrow had pierced his side, and gradually,
    Ilaganiq weakened and died.

*The men then retrieved the skins they had placed in the craft—
And also those taken by Ilaganiq.*

*Ilaganiq was in the memory of his mother
    for many days when he failed to return.
She wondered how she would continue to live without her son
    who had provided for her very well.
The mother learned how Ilaganiq had died and said,
    "This land that had provided us so well—
    It will be in the hands [of] others after I pass on."
The thought made her jealous of those
    who will certainly settle the land after her passing.
She did not want anyone to have the same comforts
    that she had.
No one [at her place] needed to travel long distances
    to return successful from a hunt in the land or on the sea.
She pondered for many days on what could be done.*

*One morning in the gathering light—
She searched for a mitten that would suit
    the purpose of her thoughts.
On finding such a mitten, she walked to the beach.
She filled the mitten with dry sand
    while singing an ancient song.
After completion of this minor chore,
    the woman walked to the edge of the waters.
She was talking alone, speaking a chant
    as the mitten disappeared into the depths.
The north wind was blowing.
The current carried the mitten, spilling its contents
    as it rolled on the bottom of the waters of the lagoon.
The current, forced by the wind,
    ferried the mitten along the lagoon bed—
It emptied itself as it rolled along.
The waters were deep—*

*But beginning from that day...
Shallow water became extreme for people
    traveling in those waters.*

*You can encounter extremely shallow water
    from the point [Nuvua] to the mouth of the Pittaq River.
The waters slightly north of the Niglanaqtuuq River
    near its mouth—
They are just a vast sandbar when the tide is very low.
The waters below the Pittaq River become extremely shallow
    but do not entirely empty at ebb tide.
This began after Ilaganiq's mother sank the mitten
    bearing the sand into the water.
The waters in the area began to get shallow
    after that time.
That is why there is shallow water there...*

~ Gideon K. Barr Sr. (1988, 1991)

Inupiaq throwing board. ~ Photo by Chris Arend, courtesy of Anchorage Museum of History and Art (82.069.001).

*This man Ilaganiq, ...he prefers to swim. He's a great swimmer when he can
  drag along a whale from Espenberg to Krusenstern site,
    just by dragging it ...*
He can swim along with a whale. And he always brings his whale across to his sister...
He brings a whale across to his sister's camp. He prefers swimming much more than using his qayaq.
  ~~ Gideon K. Barr Sr. 1988.

Painting by James Kivetoruk Moses.
~~ Photo by Trevor Roehl, courtesy of Alaska State Museum (VA-537).

*In the waters near Ipnaziaq (Deering) near the cliffs called Taugaaluuvik,
there was an animal that lived
in the deep waters there, just offshore.*

~ Gideon K. Barr Sr. 1991.

Painting by James Kivetoruk Moses.
~ Photo by Trevor Roehl, courtesy of Alaska State Museum (VA-535).

Ilaganiq, a Folktale -- 135

Cape Espenberg was just a floating ground

    with deep water under it.

And so, the mother didn't want the people

    to have an easy way of hunting, here at Espenberg,

    at the tip of Espenberg where Ilaganiq's home is.

Right after the ocean froze up,

    she filled her mitten

The one that has fur, which is made out of Caribou skin.

She filled her mitten with dry sand,

    and when the wind was blowing northwest,

    she talked with this mitten:

        "Wherever you travel, this sand will be working out

        from inside the mitten, and it will start dripping out,

        and wherever you travel, the [sea] that you went through

        will become shallow."

That's how the story is on this Ilaganiq.

When the woman's son was killed, that's when she made

    all of this shallow.

The tip of Espenberg, the Espenberg area

    all became solid ground and became shallow.

Aerial view of Cape Espenberg, August 1993. ~~ Photo by James Magdanz.

~~ Gideon K. Barr Sr. 1988.

The largest whale that Ilaganiq caught
    with hunting from a qayaq..
That's the largest whale he has bagged.
So he took the head off, and one side of the jawbone,
    and put it on top of the ground --
So his ancestor's were able to see
    how big a whale he caught from his own qayaq.

~~ Gideon K. Barr Sr. 1988.

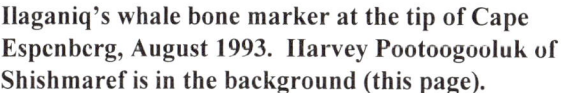

Ilaganiq's whale bone marker at the tip of Cape Espenberg, August 1993. Harvey Pootoogooluk of Shishmaref is in the background (this page).
~~ Photos by James Magdanz.

Construction detail of Ilaganiq's whale bone marker or cairn, August 1993. ~ Photo by James Magdanz.

(Opposite page)
Gideon's father, Makaiqtaq, and uncle, Sublaq, moved Ilaganiq's whale bone marker back from the eroding edge, as did their ancestors, to preserve this important landmark. Ilaganiq's marker is again threatened by erosion, August 1993. ~ Photo by James Magdanz.

Gideon Barr's nephew Fred Goodhope Jr. and grandnephew Fred Goodhope III are assisted by NPS surveyor Peter Richter, chief ranger Greg Dudgeon, and others, in moving Ilaganiq's whale bone away from the eroding bank edge, August 1996. ~ Photo by Jeanne Schaaf.

Fred Goodhope Jr. inspects Ilaganiq's whale bone marker after moving and reconstructing it, ensuring that it was put back together retaining the same directional orientation as before. NPS employees Jeanette Cross, Charles Olin, and Jason Oxereok are in the background, August 1996. ~~ Photo by Jeanne Schaaf.